GROWING AND LEARNING

The Playful Preschooler

130+ Quick Brain-Boosting Activities for 3- and 4-Year-Olds

By
Becky Daniel

D1479927

Illustrations by
Linda Hohag

Publisher
Instructional Fair • T.S. Denison
Grand Rapids, Michigan 49544

PAR
j649.58
DAN

Instructional Fair • TS Denison

All rights reserved. No part of this publication may be reproduced, stored in a retrieval system, or transmitted in any form or by any means, electronic, mechanical, photocopy, recording, or otherwise, without the prior written permission of the publisher. For information regarding permission write to: Instructional Fair • TS Denison, P.O. Box 1650, Grand Rapids, MI 49501.

About the Author ....

Becky Daniel is a parent, teacher, author, and editor—four distinctive yet interrelated professions. After graduating from California University at Long Beach, she taught kindergarten through eighth grade. When she began her family, she left the classroom to care for her first daughter and to pursue a career in writing at home.

Now the mother of three children—Amy, Sarah, and Eric—she edits a magazine and writes educational books from her home in Orcutt, California. Over the past 25 years she has written over 200 educational resource books.

She is also the author of a picture book, *Prince Poloka of Uli Loko,* a Hawaiian story for children, and *I Love You Baby,* a parenting book. In 1989 she was honored to have her biographical sketch and a list of her earlier works featured in Volume 56 of *Something About the Author.*

Credits ....

Author	Becky Daniel
Inside Illustrations	Linda Hohag
Project Director	Debra Olson Pressnall
Editors	Debra Olson Pressnall & Karen Seberg
Cover Art Direction/Design	Terri Moll
Graphic Layout & Icon Illustrations	Mark Conrad
Cover Photograph	© EyeWire

ISBN:1-56822-955-0
Growing and Learning: The Playful Preschooler
©2000 Instructional Fair • TS Denison
A Division of Instructional Fair Group, Inc.
A Tribune Education Company
3195 Wilson Drive NW, Grand Rapids, MI 49544

All Rights Reserved • Printed in USA

Dear Parents,

Being a parent to a preschooler is one of the most challenging things you will ever do. In the next few years, your child will master skills to meet nearly all of his own needs. With these new skills will come independence and self-confidence. Now, instead of being there to meet his every need, you must step back and let your child do it on his own.

You will see an abundance of experimentation happening. Watch when your child is bathing, and you will see her testing the water to see what floats and what sinks. When you uses tools in the garage, your child will probably be right there asking how everything works. When you are cooking in the kitchen, your preschooler may want to watch, taste, and smell everything. Preschoolers generally like to help with daily chores and shopping for groceries. Although it may take a great deal of time to let your child explore, experiment, and examine everything, it is the best way she can acquire knowledge. Your most important contribution to this hands-on learning will be furnishing materials for experimenting, providing enriched experiences, and praising all attempts to learn.

The simple games and activities in *Playful Preschooler* were created to help you build upon what your child can already do and enrich his intellectual growth. Your home provides a wealth of opportunities for learning. Putting puzzles together and building with blocks are excellent eye-hand coordination activities, as well as buttoning and unbuttoning clothes and lacing shoes. Making a sandwich or setting the table are learning experiences, too. With a little direction, every-day happenings can become valuable learning experiences.

There is no best way to present the activities herein. How you use the learning games will depend upon your own unique child. The important thing to remember is to praise her every attempt and accomplishment. Be positive and complimentary. You have the power to hold up a positive mirror to your preschooler—one that will reflect how capable and intelligent she is. Your attentive words and encouragement will help your child feel worthwhile and capable of learning.

Sincerely,

Becky Daniel

TABLE OF CONTENTS

INTRODUCTION

The Value of Play 6

PLAYING WITH YOUR THREE-YEAR-OLD

Fingers 'n' Thumbs
Fine Motor Development

Contemplate/Milestones 8
General Tips.. 9
Unzip Me 10
Finger Paint with Pudding 11
Shaving Cream Tracings 12
Confetti Factory..13
Picnic Collages 14
That's Me..15
Jelly Beans...16
Feeding Mommy 17
Ice Cream Cones...18
Building Sand Ponds....................................19
Making Necklaces 20
Bake a Cake 21
Pinch and Pat..22
Keeping Track..23

Ready, Set, Go!
Gross Motor Development

Contemplate/Milestones 24
General Tips..25
Hide-and-Seek...26
I Jump..27
Ring-a-Ring-a Roses 28
Hop with Mom 29
Tag..30
Racing Games 31
"Snowball" Fights..32
Catch It! 33
Kick 'n' Go! 34
Egg Rolls 35
Hot Foot 36
Beep, Beep 37
Whirl the Hoop 38
Keeping Track..39

Say What?
Language Development

Contemplate/Milestones 40
General Tips..41
Silly Sounds 42
Old King Cole 43
Old MacDonald's Farm 44
What's That? 45

Tongue Twisters...46
Finger Plays..47
Sorting Stuff...48
How Does This Look?...................................49
Opposites 50
Mother, May I?..51
Talking About Fears 52
Faces I Wear 53
Rhyme Time 54
Keeping Track..55

Cross My Heart
Social/Emotional Development

Contemplate/Milestones 56
General Tips..57
Let's Cooperate...58
Sharing 59
Bake Cookies..60
In One Minute 61
Let's Pretend...62
Real or Make-Believe? 63
Imaginary Friends 64
Dress Up 65
The Monster Mash 66
Breathe and Blow 67
Don't Cry, Baby 68
Keeping Track..69

Thinkercizes
Cognitive Development

Contemplate/Milestones 70
General Tips..71
Run to the Tree...72
Paper Collages..73
Hello, Sun—Good Night, Moon 74
Toy Parade 75
Finish the Rhyme 76
Workbench 77
Touch Together 78
Little or Big? 79
Sorting Jelly Beans 80
Shape Up! 81
Sorting by Attributes 82
Not Now—Later 83
Just Joking 84
Star Light, Star Bright...................................85
Out and About! 86
The Nose Knows 87
Keeping Track..88

PLAYING WITH YOUR FOUR-YEAR-OLD

Hands, Fingers, Thumbs
Fine Motor Development

Contemplate/Milestones 90
General Tips...91
Dressing Relay 92
Lace the Boot 93
Inside the Lines..94
Paint the "Town" Red 95
Sandpaper Shapes 96
Sandpaper Alphabet Cards 97
Drawing the Family 98
Snowperson...99
Scissor Hands 100
Dress-Up Lunch..101
Bake an Apple Pie 102
Instant Pudding 103
Soup's On! 104
Appetizers 105
Sandwiches 106
Keeping Track 107

All By Myself
Gross Motor Development

Contemplate/Milestones 108
General Tips...109
Drop Ball...110
Hopscotch 111
Jumping Jack 112
Catch with a Mitt 113
Wall Tennis 114
Bull's-Eye Games 115
Skip to My Lou 116
Wild Pony 117
Blue Bells 118
Move to the Music 119
One Step Up 120
Swing Up High...121
Teeter-Totter 122
Jungle Gym Fun 123
A Movie–Of Me? 124
Keeping Track 125

Chatter Boxes
Language Development

Contemplate/Milestones 126
General Tips...127
Move It! 128
Teddy Bear 129
Sing a Song of Sixpence..130

Twisting Tongues...131
Crooked Sixpence 132
Little Miss Muffet..133
What Would You Do? 134
How?..135
Name the Ways 136
How Many Fish?...137
When?..138
Super Star 139
Where Do You Live?...140
How Many Ways?...141
Sing a Song 142
Keeping Track 143

Flights of Fancy
Creative/Imaginative Development

Contemplate/Milestones 144
General Tips 145
Elephant Jokes 146
Dancing Hands 147
Circus Acts 148
Billy Goats Gruff 149
The House That Jack Built......................................150
It's a Zoo 152
Having a Party 153
Puppet Plays 154
Dancing Fingers 155
Clay Day 156
Paper Weavings 157
Cut and Pasting 158
Keeping Track 159

Think Tank
Cognitive Development

Contemplate/Milestones 160
General Tips 161
Name That Color 162
When?..163
Before and After 164
Naming the Alphabet...165
Alphabet Break 166
Tell Me the Story...167
Word Cards 168
Buckle My Shoe 169
Counting Rhymes...170
Time Out!...171
Whispering Voices 172
Take Care 173
Peer Pressure 174
Field Trips 175
Keeping Track 176

THE VALUE OF PLAY

For preschoolers, everything they do is learning. Adding fun to the doing and learning will make even the tedious seem like a game. The more your child plays and does, the more opportunities she has for finding favorites. Imagine if you will, what would have happened if Wolfgang Amadeus Mozart's family had never set him on a piano bench and placed his little hands on the keys? Nothing. What a loss that would have been for the world. One of your most important jobs as a parent is to find out what natural talents lie within your child.

When a child is born, he has over a hundred billion brain cells. Through play, trillions of synapses develop connecting these hundred billion cells in the brain. Each time your preschooler plays a game, listens to music or stories from picture books, and interacts with you, new synapses develop and the child's intellect is enhanced. Play, although it sounds simple, must be taken seriously. Play is your child's work!

Physically, a preschooler develops well-balanced, fine- and gross-motor skills during recreation. Toys are not just for fun. It is no accident that down through history, in all cultures, toys are a part of early childhood. Games with equipment teach the learner how to manipulate and like the old adage says, "Practice makes perfect." Mother Goose rhymes, musical games, and dancing about is play with rhythm and rhyme that orchestrates balance, coordination, and grace.

Emotionally, play is therapeutic. Since play is a natural medium for self-expression, it provides the preschooler with a safe space to experience, express, and celebrate feelings. In play, the child is given the opportunity to "play" out his accumulated feelings of tension, frustration, insecurity, aggression, fear, bewilderment, confusion. The more difficult and less obvious advantage of play is that it allows a child a place to learn how to handle anger and aggression. Although this is a long process, expressing turmoil openly in socially acceptable ways is vital for a child's emotional well-being. As a bonus, through play, children develop a sense of humor and an ability to show empathy to others. Emotionally speaking, play is vital to mental health and stability. Playing in play groups gives preschoolers the opportunity to learn social skills: sharing, taking turns, and cooperation. Patterns of behavior, acceptable ways to interact, and ways of playing safely are also part of this whole socialization process.

Creativity is a tremendous gift with which human beings are born. Unfortunately, instead of being nurtured, often imaginations are stifled. As parents and caregivers of young children, we must remember: in fantasy play, children are given a stage on which they can spotlight their creative nature. Children imagine whole scenarios and assimilate their learning through fanciful make–believe. Symbolic play, in which toys and dolls are used, allows children an opportunity to practice every possible social situation. They can rehearse all the different roles and experience being whatever they choose. This exploratory play and experience with others is a prerequisite for the child to accomplish a positive self-image. It is through fantasy play that youngsters develop their sense of humor, practice empathy, and celebrate compassion.

Everyone senses on some level that the ability to be spontaneous and to play is a basic need and an important characteristic of healthy human beings. However, not everyone can channel this force for ultimate health and happiness. Unfortunately, learning to play is something we must do as children; if we do not learn how to play as a youngster, often it is a skill that cannot be learned as an adult. As parents and caregivers of young children, I urge you to teach your child how to use her brain, body, emotions, and imagination as vehicles for celebrating her higher self. When you teach your child to play, you are showing her the path of intellectual, social, and emotional transformation—a path which ultimately leads to self-actualization!

  © Instructional Fair • TS Denison

PLAYING
With Your Preschooler
Three Years Old

Fingers 'n' Thumbs

Fine Motor Development

Contemplate

During the preschool years, children will master many complicated fine motor skills needed for their independence. At this age, children develop both the muscular control and the concentration needed to use precise finger and hand movements. Your preschooler's spatial awareness is developing too, so he will be able to set up detailed play settings with miniature plastic people, build towers of bricks, put together jigsaw puzzles with five or more large pieces, and draw pictures of people with three to six body parts.

With your child's growing independence will come a strong desire and need for refined eye-hand coordination. Three-year-olds often want to do everything for themselves. Even if it takes a long time and the child becomes frustrated, a three-year-old needs practice performing self-care tasks like brushing teeth, getting dressed and undressed, eating, etc. As your youngster learns to feed himself and drink from cups and glasses, he will probably make big messes. Be patient—the only way he will learn is to practice. The games in this chapter offer ways to help three-year-olds practice some fine-motor skills. Keep in mind that abilities vary widely with preschoolers. In the coming year, your child will learn some of the following to a certain degree, but he may not master each one.

Fine Motor Milestones: Three Years

- ◆ Will learn to unzip a zipper
- ◆ Will learn to use fingers with control as in finger painting designs
- ◆ Will learn how to trace basic shapes (circle, square, triangle)
- ◆ Will learn how to use blunt child-sized scissors
- ◆ Will learn how to use a glue stick
- ◆ Will draw people with three to six body parts
- ◆ Will learn to color in areas of a picture
- ◆ Will learn how to use eating utensils
- ◆ Will learn how to eat foods like ice cream cones
- ◆ Will learn how to pour liquid from a pitcher
- ◆ Will learn to string large wooden beads onto a shoelace
- ◆ Will learn to use some simple kitchen utensils
- ◆ Will learn how to make balls and cubes with clay

   © Instructional Fair • TS Denison

 ## General Tips

Three-year-olds are especially interested in tools. They generally want to know how things work. Craft tools and materials such as scissors, hole punch, clay, paint, paintbrushes, crayons, chalk, and sand will provide hours of enjoyment and contribute immensely to your preschooler's fine-motor development.

Sandboxes and tubs of water are very educational for children this age. Sand and water provide an excellent setting for measuring and discovering scientific principles such as *buoyancy*. Sand and water also give children an opportunity to get in touch with nature and play in a soothing, calm way. For sand and water play, include plastic measuring cups and spoons, plastic buckets and shovels, seashells, gemstones, sponges, etc.

Another opportunity preschoolers have for practicing fine-motor skills is helping with household chores. If your preschooler begins showing an interest, let her help you. Washing a table will teach your child many skills. First, she has to *think* about washing the table. Then she *feels* the washing of the table as she moves the cloth in a large, circular movement. Every step of the task is loaded with learning experiences. When she is finished and she stands back to admire her work, she will glean much self-satisfaction. If your child wants to help you with small jobs around the house, show her how to do them, and then let her find her own satisfaction.

Household tasks that some preschoolers enjoy include:
- Washing and drying a table/counter top
- Washing and tearing lettuce leaves
- Scrubbing vegetables like potatoes and carrots with a scrub brush
- Stirring batter or juice with a large wooden spoon
- Buttering bread or toast
- Kneading dough
- Slicing peeled bananas (using a plastic knife)
- Drying plastic bowls, dishes, and cups
- Folding napkins
- Putting water/dry pet food in a bowl for the pet
- Unwrapping cheese slices
- Putting bread or crackers in a basket

Most youngsters take great pride in being able to contribute to the needs of the family. Never redo a task your child has worked hard performing. Praise all her attempts to be of help.

Unzip Me

. . . Zip-a-dee-doo-dah, Zip-a-dee-day!
Wonderful feeling, wonderful day.
—Walt Disney's movie "Song of the South"

Overture

Most three-year-olds are interested in learning how tools such as zippers, scissors, and eggbeaters work. Because your preschooler now has the fine motor skills necessary to manipulate and use tools in appropriate ways, he will probably enjoy using tools.

Performance

Play: To help your preschooler learn how to unzip a large zipper, play "Unzip Me."

What you will need: Adult-sized jacket with a zipper

How to play: Put on the jacket and zip it up. Place your preschooler on your lap facing you. Ask him to help you unzip the jacket. At first, guide his hand in moving the zipper down. Zip it up again, and have him try to unzip it with less assistance. Repeat giving him less and less assistance until he can handle the zipper on his own. It may take several sessions for him to learn how to unzip the jacket. Zipping a jacket up will take even greater eye-hand coordination. This game can be played waiting in a doctor's or dentist's office, etc.

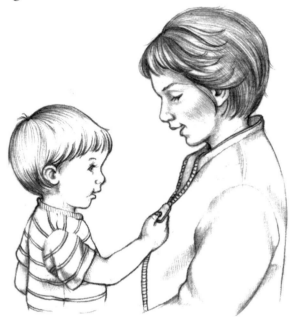

Finale

When teaching your child to zip or unzip, sing the song "Zip-a-dee-doo-dah." Put a jacket or coat with a zipper down the front on your child. Help him unzip the jacket. Then zip it up again. Give less and less assistance until he can unzip the jacket alone. After unzipping, teach him how to unlatch the zipper at the very bottom. Zipping up is much more difficult than zipping down.

Encore

Children this age like to try buttons, snaps, hooks, and buckles using frames, dressing books, or dressing dolls. Look for toys specially designed for teaching the fine-motor skills needed for self-care, such as eating and dressing. On other occasions, introduce your preschooler to lacing, stringing, and tying by practicing with an old shoe.

© Instructional Fair • TS Denison

Finger Paint with Pudding

Apple pie, apple pudding, and apple pancake,
All begins with "A."

Overture

At age three your preschooler is developing both the muscular control and the coordination needed to do precise finger and hand movements. Watch, and you will see that she is now able to move her fingers independently or together.

Performance

Play: To help your preschooler learn how to use her fingers in a controlled way, encourage her to finger paint with pudding.

What you will need: Vanilla pudding (colored with a few drops of food coloring), slick glossy paper

How to play: Instant pudding makes great finger paint. After it sets, add food coloring to vanilla pudding to make primary or secondary colors. When the paint is pudding, its fun to lick fingers. Begin by seating your child at a table or desk where she can work in a comfortable position. A high chair can be used if the eating tray is large enough to hold the paper. Wet the paper slightly. Place a few spoonfuls of pudding paint on the paper. If she does not know how to finger paint, show her how to move the paint around on the paper with her fingers. Try several different colors in the pudding to see which one she likes best.

Finale

Use the nursery rhyme to introduce your child to drawing circles. Say the nursery rhyme, and have her move fingers in circles to represent the "pies" and "pancakes."

Encore

You can also recite the nursery rhyme if you want to introduce the lowercase letter "a" to your child. Three-year-olds should not be concerned with learning the letters of the alphabet, but occasionally, in informal ways, introducing one letter at a time can be enjoyable. As you recite the nursery rhyme, show her how to turn one of the circles (pies or pancakes) into the lowercase "a" by adding a straight vertical line on the right side.

Shaving Cream Tracings

Robert Rowley rolled a round roll round,
A round roll Robert Rowley rolled round.
Where rolled the round roll
Robert Rowley rolled round?
—Traditional Rhyme

Overture

Watch, and you will see your three-year-old developing good eye-hand coordination. At age three he will be learning how to get his fingers to move the way his brain is telling them to move.

Performance

Play: To introduce your preschooler to tracing the basic shapes—circle, square, and triangle—have him draw in foamy shaving cream.

What you will need: Aluminum foil or tabletop, can of foamy shaving cream

How to play: Put some shaving cream on the surface, enough to cover it with a thin coat. Show your child how to use his index finger to draw a circle, square, or triangle in the shaving cream. Encourage him to trace the shape. As he is tracing the shape, say the name of the shape. Then rub the surface smooth and trace a different shape.

Finale

Another way to have your preschooler trace the three basic shapes is to cut them from cardboard. Show your preschooler how to trace the edges of the shapes with his index finger. As he is tracing a shape, name it for him. Describe the way his finger is moving. Encourage him to begin at the top of each shape when tracing. For example, when tracing a triangle you might say, "Down. Across. Up." When he gets very good at the game, present all three shapes at once. Give directions such as:

- ◆ Trace the circle with your finger.
- ◆ Trace the shape that goes round and round.
- ◆ Trace the triangle with your finger.
- ◆ Trace the shape that goes down, across, up.

Follow up with a guessing game using the cardboard shapes. Have your child close his eyes and hand him one of the shapes. Tell him to trace the edges of the shape. Place it back on the table with the other two shapes. Then have him open his eyes and point to the shape he thinks he was holding.

Encore

Another tracing game involves using five or six familiar household objects such as: book, cup, spoon, paper plate, etc. Place the objects on a table in front of your child. Discuss each one. Then ask your child to close his eyes. Place one of the objects in his hands. Have him trace the edges of the object. Then take it from him and place it back on the table with the other objects. When he opens his eyes, he is to point to, pick up, or name the object he was holding.

         © Instructional Fair • TS Denison

Confetti Factory

Clip, clip,
Snip, snip,
Don't slip.

Overture

Because your three-year-old can move each of her fingers independently or together, she has the coordination needed to use tools such as scissors. A pair of scissors is often a favorite tool for preschoolers. Watch how your child uses a pair of scissors, and you will see some of her new fine motor skills.

Performance

Play: To teach your preschooler how to use scissors, practice with blunt-ended scissors.
What you will need: Blunt-ended scissors, various colors of 3" by 8½" (76 x 216 mm) strips of construction paper, small shoe box
How to play: The first time your child attempts to use a pair of scissors, the goal will simply be to open and close the blades. Teach your child how to hold the scissors at a right angle to the paper. Tell your child you are going to be making confetti. Show her how to use the scissors to cut the strips into three pieces. Cut each strip twice so the pieces will be nearly square. Put the pieces in the shoe box. When she has cut several dozen pieces, use them like confetti. The large size makes it easy to pick up all the pieces. Picking up the confetti is excellent fine-motor practice for your child. Later, decorate the outside of the shoe box to look like a factory with a door and windows. Keep the colorful squares in the box with the scissors. On other occasions, cut up new colors until your child has a good assortment of confetti. Save the confetti and take it to a football game or parade.

Finale

Encourage your preschooler to use the scissors to cut strips of paper into tiny pieces. Place the different colors in separate containers such as paper cups. Then use the paper pieces to make a mosaic. Draw large, simple shapes like a circle, triangle, and square on a sheet of paper. Use a paintbrush to cover one shape with a half-water-and-half-white-glue mixture. Dump on one color of confetti. Let it dry. Shake off the excess paper confetti. Then use the paintbrush to apply the white glue mixture inside another shape. Let your child sprinkle a different color of confetti inside the shape. Let it dry. Shake off the excess confetti. Then fill in the last shape with the glue mixture. Again, let your child sprinkle on a third color of confetti. Allow it to dry and then shake off the excess confetti. Hang the paper mosaic in your home where everyone can admire the creation.

Encore

Use scissors to cut "paper lace." Fold a sheet of white paper once horizontally and once vertically. Show your child how to cut little pieces off the edges. Unfold the paper, and behold the "paper lace." Also, encourage your child to use scissors to cut fringes around the edges of large sheets of construction paper. Color the papers with markers and use them for place mats.

Picnic Collages

A glass of milk and a slice of bread,
Ants on the blanket, butterflies overhead.

Overture

Watch your three-year-old doing crafts, and you will see him mastering many precise finger and hand movements.

Performance

Play: To help your three-year-old learn how to use a glue stick, make "Picnic Collages."
What you will need: Primary scissors, white dinner-size paper plates, food magazines or supermarket ads, glue stick, blanket
How to play: Spread the blanket out on the living room rug or outside on the grass. Place the craft supplies on the blanket. Talk to your child about picnics. Discuss favorite picnic foods. Talk about pictures of foods you find in the magazines and ads. Have your child choose his favorite foods and clip pictures for the collage. Then show your child how to use the glue stick. Attach the foods to the paper plates. Make several different plates of food. Arrange the plates on the blanket and pretend to have a picnic.

Finale

Discuss the ways different foods taste: salty, sweet, and sour. Cut out pictures of sour foods in the magazines. Glue the pictures to a paper plate. Then look for some pictures of sweet foods and glue these foods to another plate. Finally, cut out some pictures of salty foods, and make a plate of salty foods, too. Place all the plates on the blanket. Ask your child to hand you the plate of sweet foods. Next ask for the sour foods. Talk about the flavors of the foods and pass them back and forth.

Examples:
◆ I will trade you this plate of sweets for some salty snacks.
◆ Pass me the plate with the sour pickles.
◆ Which plate has the sweet desserts on it?
◆ Which plate of food would you most like to eat?

Encore

Make a variety of paper plate collages. Make one for breakfast—eggs, toast, etc. Make one with a typical lunch—sandwich, apple, cookie, etc. Also create a collage of foods that your family eats at dinner. Name each plate: Breakfast, Lunch, or Dinner. Talk about the plates of food. Ask your child to hand you the plate with lunch on it. Other categories for making food collages and conversations might include:
◆ Snacks
◆ Favorite foods
◆ Foods of one color

  © Instructional Fair • TS Denison

That's Me

Polly, Dolly, Fred, and Molly,
All are pretty and jolly.

Overture

Count the number of details included in your three-year-old's self-portraits, and you will observe advancing skills. In the beginning months she may only include a head and body, but in the months to come she will add arms, legs, facial features, hair, fingers, toes, etc., to her drawings.

Performance

Play: To encourage your child to draw pictures of people, begin by having her draw self-portraits.

What you will need: Paper, crayons

How to play: Encourage your preschooler to draw pictures of herself. Do not show her how to do it. After she makes a drawing, ask her to tell you about it. Do not try to guess who was drawn in the picture or name the details in the picture. Appreciate the fact that the arms may extend from the neck and the legs may not end with feet. Let your child define the lines and circles she draws. In the beginning, her pictures of people will have as few as two or three body parts. As she matures, she will begin to add more details. When she begins adding facial features, hair, and fingers, praise her. Have her do this task in a large drawing pad at least once a month. Date each picture. Watch how her drawings become more detailed each time.

Finale

If your preschooler enjoys drawing stick people, encourage her to make drawings of the family. Ask her to tell you about each person in the picture. Feelings of belonging to a family are often enhanced by creating pictures of the immediate family.

Encore

Create a life-sized cutout doll of your preschooler. Have her lie on a long sheet of paper such as butcher paper or wide shelf paper. With feet slightly parted and arms extended a bit, have her lie very still. Use a pencil to draw around her outline. Cut out the shape. Cut up old clothes and glue them to the figure. Encourage your child to add facial features and yarn hair. Hang the cutout in your child's bedroom or another place where she can admire her life-sized paper doll.

Jelly Beans

Red, blue, yellow, green
Big, fat jelly beans.

Overture

Watch your three-year-old using crayons and coloring books, and you will probably see him struggling to stay within the lines. Although coloring books somewhat limit creativity, they do provide an opportunity for the child to practice eye-hand coordination. Filling in specific areas with certain colors is good fine-motor practice. Use coloring books sparingly and more often than not, provide your child with blank paper and crayons so he will use his imagination when coloring.

Performance

Play: To encourage your child to color certain areas of a picture, play "Jelly Beans."

What you will need: Paper, crayons, jelly beans (optional)

How to play: Draw three or four large jelly bean shapes (3–6 inches or 76–152 mm) on a sheet of paper. Tell your child that they are jelly beans, and invite him to color each one a different color. Talk about the flavors of jelly beans as he works. Remember, there are no incorrect answers. Encourage your child's creativity. Examples:

◆ Red jelly beans sometimes taste like _____.
◆ What flavor do you think yellow jelly beans are?
◆ What color do you think apple-flavored jelly beans are?

If interested, finish the activity with a jelly bean treat.

Finale

On other occasions, have your child try coloring several 2–3 inch (51–76 mm) squares that you have drawn on paper. Encourage him to use a different color for each square. Try triangles, too. Do not make the challenge too difficult by having too many figures on the paper; three or four is enough. When finished, have your child cut out each colored shape. Then overlap or arrange them in a pleasant way, and glue them to another sheet of paper.

Encore

Another interesting way to have your child practice coloring within borders is to cut large, basic shapes (circles, squares, and triangles) from white construction paper. Glue the shapes to a sheet of black paper. Have your preschooler use chalk to color the construction paper shapes. It will be easier to stay within the borders of the rough paper which is slightly elevated on the black paper. The chalk coating will create interesting effects.

 © Instructional Fair • TS Denison

Feeding Mommy

One, two, three.
Mommy loves coffee, and I love tea.
How good you be.
I love Mommy, and Mommy loves me.

Overture

Watch, and you will notice that your three-year-old's self-care skills are improving daily. She can now control the way she holds utensils and tools to perform specific tasks.

Performance

Play: To help your preschooler become more proficient using eating utensils, play "Feeding Mommy."

What you will need: Pudding, yogurt, or ice cream, two bowls and spoons

How to play: Put pudding, yogurt, or ice cream in two bowls. Explain that you want your child to feed you as well as herself. No matter how long it takes or how messy it gets, let her feed you everything in your bowl. This reversal of roles will be fun for both of you.

Finale

Encourage your preschooler to use many kitchen tools such as:

- ◆ Big spoon—Stir batter.
- ◆ Spatula—Pick up cookies from a tray.
- ◆ Plastic serrated knife—Cut soft cheese into chunks.
- ◆ Measuring cups—Fill and pour.
- ◆ Rolling pin—Roll out play clay.
- ◆ Whisk—Beat eggs to make scrambled eggs.
- ◆ Strainer—Separate seashells from sand.
- ◆ Potato masher—Mash cooled boiled potatoes.
- ◆ Pots with lids—Place lids on and off the pots.
- ◆ Plastic jars with lids—Screw and unscrew the jar lids.
- ◆ Food boxes with lids—Fit lids on boxes and take them off again.

Encore

On other occasions, let your child use self-care tools to groom you.

- ◆ Hairbrush—Brush your hair.
- ◆ Comb—Comb your hair.
- ◆ Lotion—Rub on your hands.
- ◆ Soap and water—Wash your hands or feet.
- ◆ Towel—Dry your hands or feet.

Ice Cream Cones

I scream; you scream.
We all scream for ice cream.

Overture..

Watch your three-year-old eating frozen foods on a stick or in a cone, and you will see that his spatial awareness has developed quite a bit. This skill will continue to improve over the next few months.

Performance..

Play: To help your three-year-old learn how to eat frozen foods that come on a stick or in a cone, give him plenty of opportunities to practice. Serve ice cream or frozen yogurt in cones or fruit juice bars on a stick.

What you will need: Frozen food in a cone or on a stick

How to play: Most three-year-olds are no longer willing to wear a bib. However, eating ice cream cones or frozen juice bars can get messy. Make sure your child is wearing something that can get dirty. Place the child in a booster chair so he will not walk around and eat at the same time. Give him the cone or juice bar, and let him eat it on his own. Provide a wet towel for him to use to wipe his hands and face as he is eating. This is a great time to reinforce the word "cold."

Finale...

As a special treat, let your preschooler create his own banana split or ice cream sundae. Give him a bowl, ice cream, ice cream scoop, and a variety of toppings, jams, chopped nuts, can of whipped cream, cherries, etc., from which to choose. This is especially fun at birthday parties. Consider letting all of the little guests create their own treats.

Encore ....

Most three-year-olds like to dip vegetables and snacks in cheese spread or dips. To discover your child's favorite foods for dipping, at different times provide your child with various foods including:

- ◆ Tiny carrots
- ◆ Crisp green beans
- ◆ Tender celery sticks with some leaves still attached
- ◆ Broccoli and cauliflower buds
- ◆ Sticks of cheese
- ◆ Crackers
- ◆ Sliced fruits

© Instructional Fair • TS Denison

Building Sand Ponds

Little Tee Wee, he went to sea,
In an open boat;
And while afloat the little boat bended.
My story's ended.
—Traditional Rhyme

Overture

Watch your preschooler pouring water from a pitcher into a cup, and you might be surprised how carefully she can do it. Select an area for this activity where spills will not matter; this will make mastering the skill less stressful for your child. Sandboxes or water tables in preschool classrooms as well as kitchen sinks in homes are great places for three-year-olds to practice pouring water.

Performance

Play: To teach your three-year-old how to pour liquid from a pitcher without spilling, build sand ponds.
What you will need: Tub of sand or sandbox, plastic bowls, small plastic pitcher, water
How to play: Show your preschooler how to bury the bowls in the sand so the tops of the bowls are level with the sand as if creating the foundation for an in-ground swimming pool. Next, have her use a pitcher of water to fill the "ponds." Use miniature plastic people and small cars in and around the sand ponds. When it is time to clean up, encourage your child to take out the "ponds" and pour the water in the grass or a sandy area.

Finale

You do not have to live on the seashore to make sand castles. Use pitchers of water to wet the sand enough so that it can be molded. Wet sand can be molded in plastic bowls and cups. Demonstrate how to pat the wet sand into a mold, and then tip it upside down and let it slide out of the mold.

Encore

On other occasions, make mud pies. It's fun and creative play. Provide a plastic pitcher of water, small aluminum pie pans, wooden spoons, several plastic bowls in various sizes, scoop, and a pile of dirt. Show your child how to scoop dirt into a bowl, pour water from the pitcher into the dirt, and stir to make mud. Fill the little pie pans with mud and allow them to dry. If interested, have your child use a plastic serrated knife to cut the pies into pieces. Preschoolers can play endlessly with mud.

Making Necklaces

One bead, two beads,
Red beads, blue beads.

Overture

Watch your three-year-old stringing beads, and you will see even more precision in moving and using his hands. Although three-year-olds cannot always name colors, they can sort things by color.

Performance

Play: To help your preschooler learn how to string large wooden beads, play "Making Necklaces."

What you will need: Large wooden beads, extra-long, heavy shoelaces

How to play: Tie a big knot in one end of a shoelace. Put a pile of wooden beads on the floor between you and your preschooler. Show him how to string the beads on the lace.

When the lace is nearly full of beads, tie the ends together to create a necklace that he can wear.

Finale

Use stringing beads to reinforce the concept of "same color." Choose a pile of wooden beads that include only the primary colors (red, blue, and yellow). As you string a red bead on your shoelace, tell your child to string one bead in the "same color" on his shoelace. Create very simple patterns with two, then three different colors of beads. Talk about the pattern of colors. Examples:

◆ Yellow, blue, yellow, blue . . .
◆ Red, red, blue, red, red, blue . . .
◆ Red, yellow, blue, red, yellow, blue . . .

Encore

As your preschooler's eye-hand coordination improves, encourage stringing things with smaller holes on elastic thread and make bracelets.

◆ Round cereal pieces
◆ Pasta with holes
◆ Short pieces of plastic drinking straws

  © Instructional Fair • TS Denison

Bake a Cake

Bat, bat, come under my hat,
And I'll give you a slice of bacon.
And when I bake, I'll give you a cake,
If I am not mistaken.
—Traditional Rhyme

Overture

By three years of age, meals can become a shared family event for your preschooler, providing the mealtime does not drag on too long. Sitting for more than 20 minutes is difficult for most three-year-olds. Letting your child help create a dessert for the family will be fun for her and may motivate her to be more interested in the mealtime.

Performance

Play: To give your three-year-old the opportunity to use kitchen utensils, let her help you bake and decorate a cake.

What you will need: Cake mix with needed ingredients and utensils, cake frosting or icing, sprinkles for decoration

How to play: Do not use an electric mixer to mix the batter. Place the eggs and water in a big bowl. Whip them with a wire whisk. Let your child open the cake mix box and pour the mix into the bowl. Using a big mixing spoon or wire whisk, have her stir the ingredients until the mixture is smooth. You can count 200 strokes while she stirs. She will think it is a very long time; if her arm gets tired, help her out. Your three-year-old can also help you coat the pan with shortening and put the flour in it. Let her help you pour the batter into the baking pan. Bake as directed on the package. Cool slightly and remove the cake from the pan. After the cake has cooled completely, let your child help you spread on the icing. Decorate with sprinkles, edible flower petals, or candles.

Finale

Most children are fascinated with preparing foods. Encourage your child to:

- Make peanut butter sandwiches
- Spread icing on cupcakes
- Help peel bananas
- Butter toast or bread
- Peel hard-boiled eggs
- Knead bread dough
- Unwrap individually wrapped slices of cheese
- Tear lettuce leaves and make salads
- Make chocolate milk with cocoa powder

Encore

Other mealtime activities that can involve your three-year-old include:

- Coloring and cutting fringe around edges of paper to make place mats
- Folding napkins
- Setting the table
- Putting bread in a basket

Pinch and Pat

Pinch a little, pinch a lot,
Make a pretty pinch pot.

Overture ....

Watch your three-year-old creating craft objects, and you will witness creative skills emerging. For preschoolers, being able to create art objects is a big confidence booster.

Performance ....

Play: To encourage your preschooler to create balls and cubes with clay, play "Pinch and Pat."

What you will need: Clay or one of the play doughs described below

How to play: Begin by teaching your child how to roll a lump of clay into a smooth ball. Then demonstrate how to press the ball against a firm surface to make flat sides and create a cube. Rotating the ball and pressing it on a flat surface, shows your child how to turn a ball into a cube.

Finale...

To create pinch pots, begin by rolling the lump of clay into a round ball. Then show your child how to put his thumb in the center of the ball of clay to make an indentation. Pinch the opening wider while turning the ball to form a pot. Then pinch and squeeze a lot. Go around and around and soon the ball will turn into a pot. Let it air-dry.

Encore...

To make clay at home, use either of the following recipes:

Peppermint Dough
Directions: Mix together ½ cup (120 ml) cooking oil, 2 cups (474 ml) flour, 2 cups (474 ml) salt. Stir until smooth. Add a few drops of food coloring and peppermint oil to ½ cup (120 ml) water and slowly mix it into the other ingredients. Knead the mixture until smooth and pliable.

Cornstarch Clay
Directions: Mix together 1 cup (237 ml) baking soda, ½ cup (120 ml) water, and ½ cup (118 ml) cornstarch in a heavy saucepan. Cook over low heat, stirring with a wooden spoon until the mixture becomes thick. Add a few drops of food coloring. Cool and knead until smooth. Store dough in a plastic bag in the refrigerator.

© Instructional Fair • TS Denison

Keeping Track

Milestone	Date	Comments
Can unzip a large zipper		
Can use fingers to finger paint designs		
Can trace circles, squares, triangles		
Can cut with scissors		
Can use a glue stick		
Can draw people with three to six body parts		
Can color specific areas on a picture		
Can use eating utensils		
Can eat ice cream cones and juice bars		
Can pour liquid from a pitcher without spilling		
Can string large wooden beads		
Can use kitchen utensils		
Can make clay balls and cubes		

Ready, Set, Go!

Gross Motor Development

Contemplate

Play is a child's work. Each and every day, encourage your preschooler to have fun and support her gross motor play by providing appropriate toys and a safe space for her to play. Create the play and invite the child to participate, but do not lead the games. Preschoolers should experiment and lead their own games. In free play you are providing the best possible learning environment and helping your child develop many skills including gross motor skills.

Children this age seem to never stop moving. They even use their bodies to convey messages when they are speaking. Your child has more self-control, judgment, and coordination than she did a year ago; however, adult supervision is vital. Three-year-olds should not be allowed to play outside unsupervised. Although your child is learning how things work, she still will not understand the consequences of her actions. Playing with your child will not only provide the supervision she needs, it will make her play more enjoyable.

Use the games in this chapter to introduce and reinforce skills needed to practice the gross motor milestones listed below.

Gross Motor Milestones: Three Years

- ◆ Will learn to play running about games like "Hide-and-Seek"
- ◆ Will learn to play jumping games
- ◆ Will learn to hold hands with others while moving around in a circle
- ◆ Will learn to hop while standing stationary
- ◆ Will enjoy playing a variety of tag games
- ◆ Will enjoy a variety of racing games
- ◆ Will learn to throw balls overhand
- ◆ Will learn to catch large balls tossed gently
- ◆ Will learn to kick a ball rolled slowly toward her
- ◆ Will learn to roll a ball
- ◆ Will learn to stand on one foot at a time
- ◆ Will learn to walk backward
- ◆ Will learn to swing a large plastic hoop overhead

© Instructional Fair • TS Denison

 General Tips

You can do many things to encourage your three-year-old's independent behavior. Try a few of the following ideas to help him establish independence and celebrate all of his new gross-motor skills:

◆ Put a one-step platform stool near the sink in the bathroom so he can wash his hands and brush his teeth on his own.

◆ Provide child-sized furniture in the house, especially in the bedroom.

◆ Keep healthful, individually wrapped snacks where he can reach them when he is hungry.

◆ Put an expander pole in the closet and hang clothes down low so he can reach them.

◆ Put underwear and socks in a drawer where he can get to them.

◆ Sort toys in big boxes so he can take them out and put them back again.

◆ Place plastic measuring toys in a rack on the bathtub for water play.

◆ Provide time in parks where playground equipment can be used.

◆ Play ball with your preschooler.

◆ Encourage your child to play tag and racing games with siblings.

◆ Provide a source of music and encourage him to move freely.

◆ Enroll your child in a tap dance or ballet class.

◆ Engage him in gymnastic exercises.

◆ Take walks together.

Hide-and-Seek

*Ready or not,
Here I come.*

Overture ....

Watch your three-year-old moving around, and you will see that he no longer has to concentrate on the mechanics of standing, running, jumping, or walking. Most three-year-olds are coordinated enough to play running and tag games.

Performance ....

Play: To help your preschooler learn how to find hidden objects, play "Hide-and-Seek."

What you will need: No special equipment is needed to play this game.

How to play: Demonstrate how to play the game by hiding somewhere near your preschooler. Call out, "Here I am, come find me." If your child does not understand that you want him to come looking, call out his name. When he finds you, say something like this, "Now it is your turn to hide." Close your eyes and tell your child, "Go hide." Count to ten slowly. Then call out, "Ready or not, here I come." Search for your child. When you find him, say, "Now it is my turn to hide." When you hide, leave part of your foot, hand, or body showing so it is easy for him to find you.

Finale.......................................

Play "Hide-and-Seek" outside in a fenced yard. Ask family members to join in the game—the more the merrier. When you find someone, say, "I found (name the person)." Search until you find everyone. The first person found is "It."

Encore ....

Another hide-and-seek game, "Go Find," is played with stuffed animals. You and your child each need a stuffed animal. Each player hides the toy in the house for the other to find. Then say, "Ready or not, here I come." Then each player searches for what the other has hidden. After each round of play, discuss the place you hid your toy and the place you found a toy.

Examples:
◆ I found the bear *under* your bed.
◆ I hid the pig *in* my closet.
◆ Did you hide the bear *behind* the sofa?

 © Instructional Fair • TS Denison

I Jump

Here am I, little jumping Joan,
I jump with my friends, and I jump alone.

Overture

Watch, and you will notice that as soon as your preschooler masters jumping she will begin to play games that involve jumping about. A three-year-old enjoys jumping down from slightly elevated places and being caught by the parent. Holding onto the preschooler's hands is one safe way to let her practice jumping off of things.

Performance

Play: To reinforce your preschooler's efforts in jumping, play "I Jump."
What you will need: Chalk (if played outdoors) or masking tape (if played indoors)
How to play: With chalk or masking tape, mark two parallel lines about 1 yard (91 cm) long and 1 inch (25 mm) apart. Demonstrate how to jump over the space between the two lines. Take turns jumping over the lines. Use a variety of jumping techniques including:
- Jumping flat-footed with feet together
- Running and leaping
- Jumping with one leg first, then try jumping with the other leg first
- Try hopping over the lines

Finale

Use a personalized version of the rhyme with your child's name, and recite it while you jump. Example:
   Here am I, little jumping, (*Child's name*)
   I jump with my mommy/daddy, (*Hold child's hands while jumping.*)
   And I jump alone. (*Drop hands and jump.*)
Besides jumping, try leaping, running, and hopping with your child. Use chalk to draw a line, a large square, and a large circle on the sidewalk. Demonstrate different actions, and let your child imitate your moves. Use a variety of directions such as:
- Jump into the circle.
- Leap over the line.
- Sit down inside the square.
- Walk on the line.
- Hop around the square.
- Stand still inside the circle.

Encore

On other occasions, have your child climb over or crawl through boxes (cut off two ends to make tunnels) or spend time climbing on or crawling through different parts of playground equipment. These kinds of activities will increase your child's sense of balance.

Ring-a-Ring-a Roses

Ring-a-ring-a roses,
A pocket full of posies.
Hush, hush, hush,
We'll all tumble down.
　　　　　—Traditional Rhyme

Overture..

As soon as preschoolers master walking and running, they like to use their new skills to play games. Watch, and you will see your three-year-old combining all her new skills and turning them into games. Games that involve others will be her favorites.

Performance...

Play: To reinforce your child's efforts in holding hands and moving in a circle, play "Ring-a-Ring-a Roses."

What you will need: No special equipment is needed to play this game.

How to play: Holding hands, form a circle. Use the words of the song as an action game.
　　Ring-a-ring-a roses, (*Circle clockwise.*)
　　A pocket full of posies. (*Continue circling clockwise.*)
　　Hush, hush, hush, (*Stop.*)
　　We'll all tumble down. (*Tumble down.*)
Repeat and move counterclockwise. Each time you sing the verse and begin a new game, reverse the direction of the circle.

Finale..

Other nursery rhymes that can be recited while holding your child's hands and moving in a circle include:

Jockey jog, jockey jog,
Over the hills, and over the bog.
Jockey jog, jockey jog,
Man, a mile this day I've trod.

Trip and go, heave and ho!
Up and down, to and fro.
From the town to the grove,
Two and two, let us rove.
So merrily trip and go!
So merrily trip and go!

Yankee Doodle went to town,
Upon a little pony.
He stuck a feather in his hat,
And called it Macaroni.

Hickory, hickory, sucker down!
How many miles to Richmond town?
Turn to the left, and turn to the right.
And you may get there by Saturday night.

Encore..

On other occasions, have your child hold just one of your hands, and use the rhymes as marching along songs. Swing your arms merrily as you move to the rhythm of the words.

  © Instructional Fair • TS Denison

Hop with Mom

Hop with Mom, hop with Pop.
Hop, hop, hop. Now stop!

Overture ....

Watch your preschooler moving to music, and you will see a great deal of natural rhythm. Keeping a beat is more difficult than swaying to rhythm. To help your child learn how to follow a beat, use marching music.

Performance ....

Play: To help your preschooler learn how to hop, make it a game. Practice hopping with marching music.

What you will need: Marching music, comfortable shoes with rubber soles

How to play: Play the marching music. Stand facing your child. Hop to the beat of the music as your child follows these hopping movements:

◆ Hop by standing on one foot at a time. Ask her to switch to the other foot when you do.
◆ Hop by jumping up and down with both feet together.
◆ Standing on one foot, hop up then come down on both feet. Repeat.

Finale ....

Use the rhyme to hop.
   Hop with Mom, (*Hop on right foot.*)
   Hop with Pop. (*Hop on left foot.*)
   Hop, hop, hop. (*Hop three times with feet together.*)
   Now stop! (*Freeze.*)

Encore ....

Use chalk to draw a series of connecting squares on the sidewalk. Make the squares just big enough that your child's feet fit inside them. Have her try hopping in a variety of ways:

◆ Hop from square to square on one foot as the other foot is held up behind with one hand. Then use the other foot.
◆ Hop from square to square with both feet together.
◆ Hop on one foot then the other—almost like skipping in place from square to square.

Tag

Tit, tat, toe,
My first go, . . .
　　　　　　—Traditional Rhyme

Overture ....

Three-year-olds get so excited when playing games, that they forget the rules. Children this age will run wildly into the street to chase a ball or a person while playing tag. Have your preschooler play tag and ball games in a fenced area.

Performance ....

Play: To help your preschooler learn to play various versions of running and chasing games, begin by playing regular "Tag."

What you will need: No special equipment is needed.

How to play: Three-year-olds love running and chasing games. Decide who is "It." "It" chases the other player until he can tag his opponent, then the roles are switched.

Finale ....

Use varied versions of tag to play with your child including:

◆ **Stoop Tag**—Runner is safe from being tagged if he stoops down.

◆ **Flag-Tag**—Put a cloth handkerchief in the back pocket of the runner in such a way that half of it hangs out. "It" tries to pull the handkerchief away from his opponent. When he does, he puts it in his own back pocket and the opponent becomes "It."

◆ **Freeze Tag**—A runner is safe if he freezes and stands perfectly still. He cannot be tagged by "It" while standing still.

◆ **Tree Tag**—Runners must run around two trees in the chase, no cutting corners to catch the runner. "It" must overtake his opponent in order to tag him.

Encore....................................

An interesting and fun game of tag to play at night is "Flashlight Tag." Have your preschooler try to catch the beam of light from a flashlight. Move it slowly across the lawn, but just quickly enough that he cannot catch it. Move the light beam in different ways: zigzag pattern, circles, lines. When he catches the beam of light and steps on it, let him hold the flashlight and move the beam of light while you chase it.

  © Instructional Fair • TS Denison

Racing Games

One for the money,
Two for the show,
Three to make ready,
And four to go.
—Traditional Rhyme

Overture

Watch how your preschooler runs. Children this age never seem to stop. Although her level of activity may at times be annoying and distracting for you, keep in mind that it is a necessary part of her gross-motor learning.

Performance

Play: To give your preschooler practice running races, play a variety of racing games with her.
What you will need: No special equipment is needed to play racing games.
How to play: One good racing game is to name a place where you want your child to run. She races to that place and then races back.
 ◆ Race to that tree.
 ◆ Race to the porch.
 ◆ Race around the house.

Finale

Use the rhyme to signal the beginning of a race. Show fingers: "one," "two," and "three." Clap on the word "go."
 One for the money, (*Stand tall.*)
 Two for the show, (*Lean body slightly forward.*)
 Three to make ready, (*Put one foot behind to push off.*)
 And four to go. (*Go on the word "Go."*)

Encore

Three-year-olds often like to pretend they are horses. Use the following traditional rhymes about racing horses as racing games:

This is the way the ladies ride,
Tri, tre, tri, tree, tri, tre, tri, tree!
This is the way the ladies ride,
Tri, tre, tri, tree, tri, tre, tri, tree!

This is the way the gentlemen ride,
Gallop-a-trot, gallop-a-trot!
This is the way the gentlemen ride,
Gallop-a-trot, gallop-a-trot!

This is the way the farmers ride,
Hobbledy-hop, hobbledy-hop!
This is the way the farmers ride,
Hobbledy-hop, hobbledy-hop!

One to make ready,
And two to prepare,
Good luck to the rider,
And away goes the mare.

Good horses, bad horses,
What is the time of day?
Three o'clock, four o'clock,
Now fare you away!

"Snowball" Fights

Up and down, to and fro.
Trip and go, heave and ho!

Overture

Watch your three-year-old performing large motor skills, and you will see that timing is sometimes a problem. He may understand the steps to performing a skill, but not be able to perform them at the right time to be successful at his goal.

Performance

Play: To help your preschooler practice throwing overhand, pretend to throw snowballs.

What you will need: A dozen or more pairs of rolled up white socks

How to play: Stand about 8 to 10 feet (2.4 to 3 m) away from and facing your child. Put a pile of "snowballs" (rolled-up socks) beside each of you. Show him how to toss the sock overhand like a snowball. Toss the "snowballs" and try to hit each other with the rolled-up socks. Give your child time to stoop over and retrieve "snowballs." Aim for his arms and legs and not his head.

Finale

Place a large trash can 2–4 feet (61–122 cm) in front of your child. Demonstrate how to toss the "snowballs" underhand into the trash can. One at a time, hand him a "snowball" and use the rhyme to practice tossing.

Up and down, (*Wind up for the throw, hands up, hands down.*)
To and fro. (*Hand out and back like winding up to toss a baseball.*)
Trip and go, heave and ho! (*Toss one.*)

Encore

To give your preschooler plenty of opportunities to practice tossing underhand, play bowling. Set up a few clean plastic two-liter soda bottles. Toss "snowballs" to knock them down. Also try "bowling" with a beanbag, tennis ball, rubber ball, or ball of yarn.

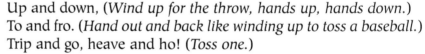

© Instructional Fair • TS Denison

Catch It!

Catch it my darling, catch it my dear.
Toss the ball, up into the air.

Overture

Watch, and you will notice that although your preschooler's coordination has improved, she still needs to make a conscious effort while manipulating a ball.

Performance

Play: To help your preschooler learn how to catch a large ball, play "Catch It!"
What you will need: Large rubber ball or beach ball
How to play: Facing each other, stand 3 feet (91 cm) away from your child. Show her how to extend her arms forward. Gently toss the ball into her arms. Demonstrate how to close her arms and bring the ball into her chest. Praise all efforts to catch the ball. Even touching the ball before it bounces is to be applauded.

Finale

Use the rhyme to signal her while playing catch.
   Catch it my darling, (*Say to signal her to extend the arms.*)
   Catch it my dear. (*Say to signal you are tossing the ball.*)
Use the rhyme to toss the ball up and catch it.
   Toss the ball up into the air. (*Say to signal her to toss it up.*)
   Catch it my darling, catch it my dear. (*Say to signal to catch it on its way down.*)

Encore

On other occasions, use small stuffed toys as balls. Toys that mold in a grasp or have long ears or a snout sticking out are easier to catch than balls. Play catch with all sorts of things, including beanbags, rolled-up socks, balls of yarn, paper wads, and inflated balloons.

Kick 'n' Go!

Great "A," little "a." Bouncing "B"!
Kick the ball away, and run to me.

Overture..

There is a wide variation of coordination skills for children this age. Some three-year-olds are quite athletic while others are more verbal and busy learning cognitive skills. Watch to see how your child is excelling—physically or verbally. Either way, the more practice with gross motor skills your child has, the more quickly he will learn.

Performance..

Play: To give your preschooler practice kicking a ball, play "Kick 'n' Go!"
What you will need: Large rubber ball
How to play: Stand facing your child about 7–8 feet (2–2.4 m) in front of him. Roll the ball gently and slowly towards him. Tell him to wait until the ball gets right in front of him before kicking it. Roll it slowly so that by the time it gets to him, it has almost stopped. Rolling it too fast will frustrate him. If a moving ball is too difficult for your child to kick, begin by having him kick a ball that is stationary. When he kicks the ball, have him run to a particular place like a tree, touch it, and then run back. Cheer him on with "Kick 'n' Go."

Finale..

Set up an obstacle course. It might be a sidewalk, taped line on a driveway, or simply a designated area in your house (like around the sofa and back). Have your child use his dominate foot to kick a small ball, such as a tennis ball, with small short kicks through the obstacle course. Later encourage him to try using his nondominant foot for kicking a ball through the obstacle course.

Encore ....

On other occasions, use a variety of things to kick along the course:
- ◆ Cardboard tube from toilet tissue
- ◆ Cat toy ball with bells inside
- ◆ Rolled-up socks
- ◆ Round large bath sponge
- ◆ Large beanbag
- ◆ Ball of yarn

   © Instructional Fair • TS Denison

Egg Rolls

Egg rolls—ten cents a dozen,
Buy some for your uncles and aunts.
Egg rolls—ten cents a dozen,
Take some home to your cousins.

Overture

Some three-year-olds can bend over and perform activities without tumbling over. Watch to see if your child can. If she cannot, play games that will encourage her to bend, stoop, and retrieve.

Performance

Play: To help your preschooler learn how to bend over and roll an object, play "Egg Rolls."

What you will need: Two large plastic eggs (the kind used to package pantyhose), rice, tape

How to play: Fill the plastic eggs half full of rice and tape them closed. Demonstrate how to bend over and roll the eggs along the ground. Have races rolling the eggs from place to place.

Finale

Challenge your child to roll other things along the floor such as:

◆ Rolled-up sock
◆ Small tennis ball
◆ Large rubber ball
◆ Paper towel roll
◆ Grapefruit
◆ Football
◆ Inflated balloon
◆ Rolled-up newspaper

Encore

On other occasions, use two large plastic balls to play "Roll 'Em." Stand facing your child about 6 feet (1.9 m) away from her. In this game, both players have a large rubber ball. Each player rolls her ball toward the other player's ball. The object of the game is to push the other person's ball back with your ball.

Hot Foot

Hop away, skip away, my baby wants to play.
My baby wants to play every day.
—Traditional Rhyme

Overture ....

Most three-year-olds have vivid imaginations. Set up a pretend game, and they will play it to the maximum. Nothing is too silly or fanciful that they will not enjoy it.

Performance ....

Play: To help your preschooler learn how to stand on one foot at a time, play "Hot Foot."
What you will need: No special equipment is needed to play this game.
How to play: Both you and your child should be barefooted. Tell him to pretend he is walking in hot sand at the beach. Demonstrate how to shift from foot to foot. Say things like "Hot! This sand is very hot. Hot cha, cha Baby!" Dance about the area.

Finale...

Use the same barefoot game to practice standing on one foot and then switching to the other foot to act out other scenarios, such as:

- ◆ Walking on ice
- ◆ Walking in prickly grass
- ◆ Walking in honey
- ◆ Walking on sharp rocks
- ◆ Walking in gooey mud
- ◆ Walking in very tall grass

Encore...

On another occasion, have your three-year-old try to hop, jump, run, and move like certain animals.
Examples:

- ◆ Rabbit—Squat and take big hops with feet together.
- ◆ Bird—Take tiny hops from one foot to the other.
- ◆ Kangaroo—Take big giant hops with feet together.
- ◆ Horse—Gallop leading first with the right foot, then the left foot.
- ◆ Turtle—On all fours, lead with right limbs and then left limbs to move forward.

© Instructional Fair • TS Denison

Beep, Beep

Beep, beep, I'm a jeep.
Beep, beep, I'm a jeep.

Overture....................................

Most three-year-olds like to pretend they are motorized vehicles.

Performance................................

Play: To help your preschooler learn how to walk backward, pretend to be a jeep.

What you will need: No special equipment is needed to play this game.

How to play: Demonstrate how to move around in straight lines like a jeep moving forward on a road. Make the horn beeping sound. When turning corners, pretend to turn an imaginary steering wheel. Then show her how to look over her shoulder and move backward as if driving the jeep in reverse.

Finale.......................................

Pretend to be other moving objects:

- ◆ Sailboat
- ◆ Airplane
- ◆ Merry-go-round
- ◆ Submarine
- ◆ Rocket blasting off
- ◆ Swinging swing

Encore.......................................

Try racing moving backward including:

- ◆ Walking backward
- ◆ Running backward
- ◆ Hopping from foot to foot backward
- ◆ Crawling backward
- ◆ Tiptoeing backward

Whirl the Hoop

Bring the hoop, and bring the ball,
Come with happy faces all.
Let us make a merry ring,
Talk and laugh, and dance and sing.

Overture

Three-year-olds still have difficulty performing tasks that they cannot see. For example, they may be able to whirl hoops in front of them, but then have difficulty performing the same trick above their heads where they cannot see the hoops. Watch your child performing a motor skill, and you will see that he watches what he is doing.

Performance

Play: To teach your preschooler how to turn a large plastic hoop overhead, play "Whirl the Hoop."

What you will need: A plastic hoop

How to play: Demonstrate how to hold the hoop overhead with two hands. Hold one hand directly behind the head and the other hand directly in front of the head. Reverse the hands putting the one behind the head in front of the head and the one in front of the head behind the head. Move the hands back and forth so that the hoop moves around in half circles, clockwise and counterclockwise.

Finale

Have your child try other overhead movements with the hoop including:
◆ Up and down—Raise and lower the hoop. Start with it shoulder high and then extend arms up straight so it is overhead. Move the hoop up and down.
◆ Side to side—Hold one arm so that it is held out to the side and the other arm is straight up; then reverse so the overhead arm becomes the arm to the side and the other arm is straight up. Move hoop side to side.

Encore

On other occasions use the hoop to move in new, fanciful ways:
◆ Try rolling the hoop while walking forward.
◆ Place the hoop on the ground and walk around the outside of it.
◆ Place the hoop on the ground, and jump in and out of it.
◆ Place the hoop on the ground, and put one foot inside and one foot outside. Hop back and forth from one foot to the other.

Keeping Track

Milestone	Date	Comments
Can play "Hide-and-Seek" games		
Can play jumping games		
Can hold hands and move in a circle		
Can hop		
Enjoys a variety of tag games		
Enjoys a variety of racing games		
Can throw overhand and underhand		
Can catch a large ball		
Can kick a moving ball		
Can roll a ball toward someone		
Can stand on one foot at a time		
Can walk/move backward		
Can maneuver a large plastic hoop overhead		

Say What?

Language Development

Contemplate

Contemplate your child's rapid language development. By three-and-a-half years, most preschoolers have a vocabulary of 300 to 1,000 words. You are your child's main language model. When you speak to her, it is best if you no longer use "baby talk." Instead, use the appropriate names for objects and body parts. Hearing correct words will make learning to speak easier for your child.

Listen to your three-year-old's speech patterns, and you may discover some sounds are missing. Until she learns all of the consonant and vowels sounds, she will not be able to form all words. Informal games that include making consonant and vowel sounds will help your child increase her vocabulary. Learning to speak while not knowing how to make all of the sounds is like trying to type a letter when some of the letters on the keyboard are missing.

Remember, children learn language at different rates. In the coming year or two, your child will master the milestones below. Use the games in this chapter to have fun with words and increase your child's speaking vocabulary.

Language Milestones: Three Years

◆ Will be able to make the sounds of most of the consonants
◆ Will be able to make the sounds of the long vowels
◆ Will be able to make the sounds of the short vowels
◆ Will learn to use 300 to 1,000 words
◆ Will speak in five- to six-word sentences
◆ Will be able to memorize very short nursery rhymes
◆ Will be able to verbalize similarities and differences
◆ Will include adjectives when talking
◆ Will understand and use antonyms
◆ Will include adverbs when speaking
◆ Will begin to use language to express fears
◆ Will begin to use language to express feelings
◆ Will be able to rhyme words

 © Instructional Fair • TS Denison

 General Tips

Encourage language development for your three-year-old by:
◆ Speaking directly to him.
◆ Giving him time to respond.
◆ Carrying on conversations with him.
◆ Offering encouragement by responding to his words.
◆ Reading to him.

Reading to your preschooler will give him the opportunity to hear words chosen especially for this age group. Three-year-olds are usually able to sit for 15 to 20 minutes or even longer to hear stories. They enjoy familiar subjects, tales with details, and less repetition than at age two. Three-year-olds especially enjoy getting involved in the storytelling. Touch and feel books are appealing to this age group. Some appropriate touch and feel books for three-year-olds include:
◆ *Pat the Cat (Golden Touch & Feel Book)* by Edith Kunhardt (Golden Books, 1984)
◆ *Pat the Bunny (Golden Touch & Feel Book)* by Dorothy Kunhardt (Golden Books, 1990)
◆ *Pat the Bunny: My Furry Friends (Golden Touch and Feel Books)* by Edith Kunhardt (Golden Press, 1994)
◆ *Pat the Puppy (Golden Touch & Feel Book)* by Edith Kunhardt (Golden Books, 1993)
◆ *Feely Bugs: To Touch and Feel* by David A. Carter (Little Simon, 1995)
◆ *Textures (Change-A-Boards)* by Joanne Barkan (Random House, 1998)
◆ *Touch and Feel: Clothes* by Deni Brown (DK Pub.,1998)
◆ *Touch and Feel: Farm* by Deni Brown (DK Pub., 1998)
◆ *Touch and Feel: Home* by Deni Brown (DK Pub., 1998)
◆ *Touch and Feel: Wild Animals* by Deni Brown (DK Pub.,1998)

Language Development Three-Year-Old

© Instructional Fair • TS Denison

Silly Sounds

"Yaup, yaup, yaup!"
Said the frog, as it hopped away.

Overture

Stimulate your child's language acquisition by making the sounds of some of the initial consonants. Keep in mind that the sounds "f," "v," "s," and "z" may remain difficult for your child until age five or six, and he may not fully master "sh," "l," "th," and "r" until age six or seven. Listen, and you will probably hear your son making the sound of a car while pushing toy cars around. Girls rarely do this, but boys nearly always do.

Performance

Play: To practice the sounds of isolated consonants, play "Silly Sounds."
What you will need: No special equipment is needed to play this game.
How to play: Introduce and reinforce some initial consonant sounds by having your child make the sounds he hears you making. Try to make just the sound of the consonant; do not include the vowel. For example: for the letter "P" do not say "paw." The sound you make should be an explosion of air between the lips. If a sound is difficult for your child to make, explain and demonstrate how he is to hold his tongue, teeth, and lips. A hand mirror may help him see if he is holding his mouth in the correct position for making the sounds.

- "P"—Final sound in "pop"
- "B"—Initial sound in "baby"
- "D"—Final sound in "bad"
- "G" and "J"—Final sound in "edge"
- "K"—Final sound in "seek"
- "M"—Sound made when something is pleasing, "mmm"
- "N"—Final sound in "on"
- "T"—Final sound in "not"

Finale

On other occasions, use all the sounds he has learned and include some of the more difficult-to-make sounds, too.

- "C," "S," "Z,"—Initial sound in "see"
- "H"—Initial sound in "hot"
- "R"—Initial sound in "roof"
- "W"—First sound in "wet"
- "F"—Final sound in "off"
- "L"—Final sound in "ball"
- "V"—Final sound in "salve"
- "Y"—Initial sound in "yes"

Encore

It has been said that the human voice is the most beautiful musical instrument in the world. When your child can make many of the sounds of the letters in the alphabet, play "Voice Band." Make a sound, one, two, or three times. The object of the game is for your child to make the correct sound the correct number of times. Give him a turn to be the leader and you follow. Make music!

© Instructional Fair • TS Denison

Old King Cole

Old King Cole was a merry old soul,
And a merry old soul was he; . . .
—Traditional Rhyme

Overture

Words are a combination of consonant and vowel sounds. To turn the consonant sounds into words, vowel sounds must be learned, too. Play games that emphasize the long and short vowel sounds. Your child does not have to know the name of the vowel or if it is the long or short sound. Just making the sounds is enough at this age. Watch your child when she is playing by herself. She will use the sounds she has learned in her games.

Performance

Play: Use the nursery rhyme, "Old King Cole" to familiarize your three-year-old with the long vowel sounds "o" and "e."

What you will need: No special equipment is needed to play this game.

How to play: Make the long "o" sound. Tell your child to make a circle with her lips and make the long "o" sound every time she hears it. Then recite the rhyme.

Old King Cole was a merry old soul,
And a merry old soul was he.
And he called for his pipe,
And he called for his bowl,

Use the next lines of the same rhyme to have your child listen for the long "e" sound. Demonstrate the long "e" sound. Then ask her to make the sound when she hears it in the rhyme.

And he called for his fiddlers three.
And every fiddler, he had a fine fiddle,
And a very fine fiddle had he.
"Tweedle dee, tweedle dee," said the fiddlers three.

Next have your child listen for both long "o" and long "e" and make those sounds as you finish the rhyme.

Oh, there's none so rare as can compare
With King Cole and his fiddlers three.

Finale

To teach the long "a" sound, have your child make the sound a horse makes, "neigh." Have your child use a hobby horse to move about while making the long "a" sound. Reinforce the long "e" sound by having her make the sound a chick makes (peep) or the sound a mouse makes (squeak.)

Encore

Reinforce long "i" and long "u" sounds by playing "Who Can?" Ask questions that can be answered with "I can" or "you can."

◆ Who can sleep in your bed? (*Child answers, "I can."*)
◆ Who can drive the car? (*Child answers, "You can."*)

Old MacDonald's Farm

Old MacDonald had a farm. E-I-E-I-O.
And on his farm he had a lamb. E-I-E-I-O.
With a baa, baa, here and a baa, baa, there.
Here a baa, there a baa, everywhere a baa, baa.
Old MacDonald had a farm. E-I-E-I-O.
—Traditional Song

Overture

Listen to your three-year-old's speech patterns, and you may discover some sounds are missing. Until he learns all of the consonant and vowels sounds, he will not be able to say all words.

Performance

Play: To practice making a variety of vowel sounds, sing "Old MacDonald's Farm."
What you will need: No special equipment is needed to play this game.
How to play: Sing the song "Old MacDonald's Farm" and substitute a variety of animals including those listed below. With your help, have your child make the different animal sounds. Emphasize the vowel sounds. Animal sounds that reinforce vowels include:

- Duck—Qu<u>a</u>ck (short "a")
- Snake—H<u>i</u>sssss (short "i")
- Lamb—B<u>aa</u>, b<u>aa</u> (short "a")
- Goose—H<u>o</u>nk (short "o")
- Cow—M<u>oo</u>, m<u>oo</u> ("oo")
- Frog—R<u>i</u>bb<u>i</u>t, r<u>i</u>bb<u>i</u>t (short "i")
- Bee—B<u>u</u>zz, b<u>u</u>zz (short "u")
- Horse—N<u>eigh</u>, n<u>eigh</u> (long "a")
- Chick—P<u>ee</u>p, p<u>ee</u>p (long "e")
- Pig—Squ<u>ea</u>l (long "e")
- Mouse—Squ<u>ea</u>k, squ<u>ea</u>k (long "e")

Finale

Without using the song, make animal sounds and have your child echo the sounds he hears. Or have him make animal sounds, and you guess the name of the animal.

Encore

Use the expression from the story "Jack and the Beanstalk" to practice the long vowel sounds. "Fe, fi, fo, fum! I smell the blood of an Englishman." Substitute different initial consonants and include the long "a" sound, and see if your child can make the sounds.

- Ba, be, bi, bo, bum!
- Da, de, di, do, dum!
- La, le, li, lo, lum!
- Ma, me, mi, mo, mum!
- Na, ne, ni, no, num!

© Instructional Fair • TS Denison

What's That?

See, see. What shall I see?
A horse's head where his tail should be.
—Traditional Rhyme

Overture

Amazing as it may sound, many preschoolers have a vocabulary of 300 to 1,000 words. Listen, and you will hear your child using new vocabulary every day.

Performance

Play: To help your preschooler learn new words, play "What's That?"

What you will need: Children's picture books, magazines, or catalogs

How to play: Place your child on your lap so she can see the pictures in the book or magazine. Point to a picture and ask "What's that?" Give her time to think of the name of the object. If she cannot name the object, give her the sound of the initial consonant. For example, if you are pointing to a picture of a basketball and she cannot name it, make the sound of the first letter or syllable—"bas." Give her time to think of the word. If she still cannot name it, give her both the first and second syllables of the word. If the word has more than two syllables, continue adding parts of the word until you have given the complete word or your child has named it. Ask her to point to the picture and say the word. The touching of the picture and naming it at the same time is an important language connection. Learning one or two new words in each setting is about all children this age enjoy; stop the game when your child is no longer interested in playing. If your child likes the game, introduce or reinforce additional words on other days.

Finale

Concentrate on new vocabulary with a theme. For example, use picture books of wild animals to teach interesting animals, clothes catalogs to teach articles of clothing, tool catalogs to teach tools and machinery, etc. If your three-year-old is especially interested in a topic, introduce many words to her so she can discuss the subject with you.

Encore

When you are out walking or riding in the car, point to things and ask, "What's that?" Challenge her vocabulary with things she can see and touch while naming the objects. The more engaging you can make her learning, the more quickly she will learn.

Tongue Twisters

She sells seashells by the seashore.

Overture

Watch your three-year-old, and you will see how he delights in saying new words. Many children this age enjoy nonsense sayings and tongue twisters.

Performance

Play: To give your child an opportunity to speak in five- to six-word sentences, teach him short tongue twisters.

What you will need: No special equipment is needed for this activity.

How to play: Teach tongue twisters a few words at a time. Then teach her a whole line. Later you can add more lines to the tongue twister. Begin with a simple one such as "She sells seashells by the seashore." Begin by teaching him how to say each separate part of the sentence. If he has trouble with any part of the sentence, do not string it together. Only when he can say all of the separate parts should you combine the parts into a sentence. When your child can say the tongue twister, try having him say it repeatedly or as fast as he can.

Finale

Other tongue twisting lines from familiar nursery rhymes to teach your three-year-old include:

- ◆ Pat-a-cake, pat-a-cake, baker's man. Bake me a cake as fast as you can.
- ◆ Rain, rain, go away. Come again another day.
- ◆ Handy spandy, Jack a-dandy, loves plum cakes and sugar candy.
- ◆ It's raining, it's pouring, the old man is snoring. (Snooooore.)
- ◆ Trip and go, heave and ho! Up and down, to and fro.
- ◆ Peter, Peter, pumpkin-eater, had a wife and couldn't keep her.
- ◆ Mary, Mary, quite contrary, how does your garden grow?
- ◆ Around the green gravel the grass grows green.
- ◆ Tip, top, tower, tumble down in an hour.
- ◆ I saw a ship a sailing—a sailing on the sea.

Encore

Tapes and CDs of nursery rhymes and children's song will give your preschooler an opportunity to hear new words and practice saying/singing them. Encourage your child to sing, by singing while you work. If you express your joy with songs and laughter, your child will learn to do the same.

© Instructional Fair • TS Denison

Finger Plays

This little pig went to market.
This little pig stayed home.
This little pig had roast meat.
This little pig had none.
This little pig cried, "Wee, wee, wee, I can't find my way home."
—Traditional Rhyme

Overture ....

Teaching your child rhymes can be great fun. With a little imagination, most rhymes can be turned into finger plays. To help your child memorize the rhymes use the one-word, one-phrase, and one-line steps as described below.

Performance ....

Play: To give your three-year-old opportunities to learn nursery rhymes, turn them into finger plays.

What you will need: No special equipment is needed for this game.

How to play: Sit on the floor facing your barefoot child. With your index finger and thumb, wiggle the appropriate toe on your child as you recite the nursery rhyme.

This little pig went to market. (*Wiggle biggest toe.*)
This little pig stayed home. (*Wiggle second toe.*)
This little pig had roast meat. (*Wiggle middle toe.*)
This little pig had none. (*Wiggle fourth toe.*)
This little pig cried, "Wee, wee, wee, I can't find my way home." (*Wiggle littlest toe.*)

Then repeat the rhyme, pausing for your child to fill in words. For example: This little ____ (pig) went to _____ (market).

Finale ....

As your child becomes more familiar with the rhyme, wiggle the appropriate toes and just give the first three words for each line. Pause so your child can give the last part of each line.

Encore ....

The final step for teaching the entire rhyme is to just wiggle each toe and have your child say the whole corresponding line on her own. Use this three-stage method for teaching other nursery rhymes to your child.

Sorting Stuff

Pease porridge hot, pease porridge cold,
Pease porridge in the pot nine days old.
Some like it hot; some like it cold.
Some like it in the pot nine days old.
—Traditional Rhyme

Overture

Watch your child playing with toys, and you will sometimes see her sorting items into piles of things that are the same.

Performance

Play: To help your three-year-old learn to sort things that are the same and different, play "Sorting Stuff."

What you will need: Big box of toys with items that can be described in one or more of the following ways:

- ◆ Soft/hard
- ◆ Round/square
- ◆ Light/heavy
- ◆ Rough/smooth
- ◆ Big/little

How to play: Ask your child to sort through the toys and make a pile of things that are soft and things that are not soft. Then put all the toys back in the box. Next have her sort the toys into a pile of things that are round and things that are not round. Repeat using the categories listed above.

Finale

Use the same toys to discuss similar/different attributes. Place two toys on the table and ask your child how they are alike. For example, you might ask, "Are both of these toys the same shape?" In the beginning, your child may not be able to verbalize the way the toys are similar/different, but she will comprehend the similarities/differences. Form questions that she can answer with a "yes" or "no." Maybe they are both *soft* or both *round* or *little*. Name attributes that the two toys have in common. Then put those toys away and choose two new ones. The more your child can verbalize the similarities/differences, the better.

Encore

On other occasions, use the same box of toys to verbalize how two toys are different. Describe the attributes that are not common to the two toys. For examples:

- ◆ Ball and a book (One is round and one is square.)
- ◆ Teddy bear and a block (One is soft and one is hard.)

Talk to your child about ways she is similar to family members and ways she is unique.

          © Instructional Fair • TS Denison

How Does This Look?

Mary had a pretty bird,
Feathers bright and yellow,
Slender legs, upon my word,
He was a pretty fellow. . . .
—Traditional Rhyme

Overture

You can help your three-year-old expand his vocabulary by providing descriptive words for common objects. Listen to discover if your child is beginning to use descriptive words.

Performance

Play: To encourage your three-year-old to include basic adjectives when talking, play "How Does This Look?"

What you will need: Toys, objects, and foods that can be described as one of the following:

- ◆ Soft/hard
- ◆ Light/heavy
- ◆ Rough/smooth
- ◆ Black/white
- ◆ Long/short
- ◆ Wet/dry
- ◆ Big/little
- ◆ Shiny/dull

How to play: Hold up an object and ask, "How does this look?" Help your child use some of the adjectives on the list to describe the toy. For example, "The teddy bear is *soft* and *black.*" Then ask, "How does this feel?" "The teddy bear is *light* and *little.*"

Finale

Teaching descriptive words happens naturally in the kitchen. When foods are involved, you can usually get a child's full attention. Have your child taste foods and ask, "How does this taste?" Help him use descriptive words for the flavors.

- ◆ Salty/bland (chips and bread)
- ◆ Spicy/bland (cinnamon cookies and sugar cookies)
- ◆ Soft/chewy (marshmallow and caramel)
- ◆ Crunchy/smooth (two kinds of peanut butter)
- ◆ Sweet/sour (two kinds of pickles)
- ◆ Hot/cold (cocoa and milk)

Encore

When speaking, include adjectives to describe things. Ask questions like:

- ◆ Do you see something that is "white" and "fluffy" in the sky?
- ◆ What is "bright" and "shiny" in the sky at night?

Opposites

Boys and girls, come out to play,
The moon doth shine as bright as day; . . .
—Traditional Rhyme

Overture

Playing games with antonyms is a good way of testing to see if your preschool comprehends certain words. Knowing the opposite meaning of a word (knowing what it does not mean) is proof that your child understands the word.

Performance

Play: To help your three-year-old learn antonyms, play "Opposites."

What you will need: Objects to demonstrate opposites: soft bear and hard metal car, ball and a square block/box, light balloon and heavy brick, wet and dry sponges

How to play: Begin by placing the objects to teach the opposites on a table. Pick up the soft toy and say, "This is *soft.*" Then pick up the car and ask, "Is this *soft*?" Ask, "What is this?" Encourage your child to include descriptive words when naming the objects. Then you might ask your child to pick up something *round*, or ask which things are not *round*. Touch and talk about the toys to teach the opposites: soft/hard, have edges (cube)/no edges (ball), light/heavy, wet/dry.

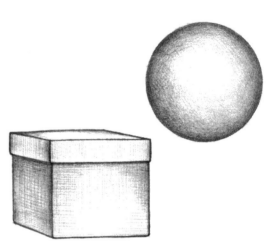

Finale

On other occasions, use toys and objects for comparison including:
- Rough/smooth (sandpaper and paper)
- Big/little (family car and toy car)
- Black/white (construction paper)
- Shiny/dull (aluminum foil and waxed paper)
- Flat/pointed (eraser and pencil)

Encore

Take the touching and learning outside. Include discussions of any of these:
- Tall/short (trees and bushes)
- Fluffy/hard (dandelion seed and stone)
- High/low (sky and ground)
- Smooth/rough (different leaves)
- Prickly/smooth (cactus and leaf)

 © Instructional Fair • TS Denison

Mother, May I?

Hop and skip, leap up high.
Gallop and jump, spring to the sky.

Overture

Watch, and you will see that your three-year-old is as active as she was at age two, but now she will be more interested in structured games. Instead of running aimlessly or flittering from one activity to another, she may want to play organized games—preferably with a partner or playmates.

Performance

Play: To help your three-year-old learn adverbs, play "Mother, May I?"
What you will need: No special equipment is needed for this game.

How to play: Have your child stand next to you. Give her directions which include adverbs. She must first ask "Mother, may I?" before she moves as directed. Include these kinds of movements and adverbs:

◆ Run "quickly" to that tree and back to me.
◆ Tiptoe "softly" to that bush and back again.
◆ "Quietly" hop on one foot.
◆ Stomp your feet "loudly."
◆ "Merrily" skip to the porch.
◆ "Slowly" tiptoe to the tree and back again.

Finale

Use the same adverbs to perform other simple tasks such as clap, sing a song, stomp, run in place, make noises, etc.

◆ Clap hands together "quickly" (softly, quietly, loudly, happily, slowly).
◆ Sing a song "quickly" (softly, quietly, loudly, happily, slowly).
◆ Stomp your feet "quickly" (softly, quietly, loudly, happily, slowly).
◆ Run in place "quickly" (softly, quietly, loudly, happily, slowly).

Encore

Provide the opportunity for your child to hear a wide range of adverbs by speaking with many descriptive words. Ask her questions that will encourage the use of adverbs, too.

◆ Describe how you ran to the tree—"slowly" or "quickly."
◆ Tell me how the dog runs—"merrily" or "clumsily."
◆ Which is your favorite way to skip—"happily" or "thoughtfully"?

Talking About Fears

*The wild things roared their terrible roars
and gnashed their terrible teeth
and rolled their terrible eyes
and showed their terrible claws. . . .*

—*Where the Wild Things Are*
by Maurice Sendak

Overture

Language is a way for three-year-olds to express fears. Talking about fears may help your child overcome his anxieties. Listen, and your child will let you know what things he fears most.

Performance

Play: To encourage your three-year-old to use language to express fears, read the book *Where the Wild Things Are* to him.

What you will need: *Where the Wild Things Are* by Maurice Sendak (Harper & Row, 1988)

How to play: Sit with your child in your lap so he can see the pictures and read the story. After you finish the book, turn to the pages with the pictures of the "terrible things." Ask your child to touch the wild things' terrible teeth, eyes, and claws. Discuss how silly they look.

Finale

Talk to your child about his own "monsters." Does he have scary dreams? What are the scary things he sees in his dreams? See if he can describe his scary thoughts. Use crayons to draw pictures of "terrible things." Then ask your child to tell you about the pictures. Ask him about the monster's color, size, the sounds it makes, etc. Make the "monster" seem more friendly by asking questions.

◆ What does the monster eat for breakfast?
◆ What does the monster's bed look like?
◆ What are the monster's favorite foods?
◆ What does the monster do on his birthday?
◆ What does the monster fear?

Encore

To provide opportunities for your child to talk about his fears, be available to listen. If your child is afraid of something, talk about it. The more he talks about the fear, the more easily he will be able to come to grips with it. Do not invalidate his fears by saying "Don't be afraid." If he is afraid, acknowledge the fear and discuss it. You might want to tell him about the things that you feared when you were a child.

   © Instructional Fair • TS Denison

Faces I Wear

When I am glad, my mouth turns up,
My eyes sparkle and glow.
When I am sad, my mouth turns down,
My tears begin to flow.
When I am excited, my face is bright;
My eyes open very wide.
When I am afraid, I close my eyes,
And crawl inside myself to hide.

Overture

Watch, and you will notice that your three-year-old wears her feelings on her face. When she is sad, you will see the sadness in her eyes. When she is happy, her eyes will dance. When she is anxious, her brow may wrinkle, and she might wear her worry on her face.

Performance

Play: To encourage your preschooler to talk about her feelings, play "Faces I Wear."
What you will need: Hand mirror
How to play: Have your child gaze into the mirror and make faces as you say the rhyme.

When I am glad, my mouth turns up,
My eyes sparkle and glow. (*Smile.*)
When I am sad, my mouth turns down,
My tears begin to flow. (*Frown or pout.*)
When I am excited, my face is bright;
My eyes open very wide. (*Make excited face.*)
When I am afraid, I close my eyes,
And crawl inside myself to hide. (*Close eyes.*)

Finale

On other occasions, use the hand mirror to have your child watch herself as she makes other facial expressions:

- ◆ Surprised
- ◆ Sad
- ◆ Scared
- ◆ Mad
- ◆ Excited
- ◆ Sleepy

Encore

You may be unaware of it, but your child is very aware of your feelings. She watches your face for signs of anxiety, approval, joy, etc. Make different facial expressions, and see if your child can name a feeling for each one.

Rhyme Time

Jack Sprat had a cat
The cat sat on a mat.
Jack Sprat had a rat
That lived in his hat.

Overture

Watch your three-year-old acquiring language skills, and you will see that each new word he learns opens up an opportunity for learning many other words. Rhyming is a fun way of introducing new words to your child.

Performance

Play: To help your three-year-old learn about rhyming words, play "Rhyme Time."

What you will need: No special equipment is needed to play this game.

How to play: When introducing this game to your three-year-old, instead of saying "rhymes with" tell your child "the ending sounds the same." Give some examples such as these easy-to-say and understand rhyming words: at, bat, cat, fat, hat, mat, pat, rat, sat. Say each word. Have your child repeat each word. Then ask questions that can be answered using the rhyming "at" words.

- ◆ What is used to hit a ball? (bat)
- ◆ What is a kitten's mommy called? (cat)
- ◆ What is a big, round, heavy cat called? (fat)
- ◆ What do you call something you wear on your head? (hat)
- ◆ What is a word that means to pet or stroke with your hand called? (pat)
- ◆ What is a little animal with little ears and a thin tail called? (rat)
- ◆ What is a little animal with big ears that flies at night called? (bat)

Finale

On other occasions, introduce additional rhyming word lists and ask questions that can be answered with one of these:

- ◆ Dog, fog, hog, log
- ◆ Bee, he, key, knee, me, she, tea
- ◆ Bus, fuss, us
- ◆ Ed, bed, fed, head

Encore

Many books authored by Dr. Seuss have wonderful rhymes. Read some rhyming Dr. Seuss books to your child including:

- ◆ *Hop on Pop*
- ◆ *Cat in the Hat*
- ◆ *Cat in the Hat Comes Back*
- ◆ *The Foot Book*
- ◆ *In a People House*
- ◆ *Great Day for Up*
- ◆ *Oh, the Thinks You Can Think!*
- ◆ *There's a Wocket in My Pocket!*

 © Instructional Fair • TS Denison

Keeping Track

Milestone	Date	Comments
Can say isolated consonant sounds		
Can say isolated long vowel sounds		
Can say isolated short vowel sounds		
Uses 300 or more words verbally		
Can speak in five- to six-word sentences		
Can say short nursery rhymes from memory		
Can verbalize similarities/differences		
Can use adjectives to describe		
Understands and uses antonyms		
Can use adverbs to describe		
Can use language to express fears		
Can use language to express feelings		
Understands and uses rhyming words		

Cross My Heart

Social/Emotional Development

Contemplate

One of the most important things you can teach your preschooler is how to have fun. When he sees you enjoying yourself, it gives him permission to enjoy life, too. Being joyful is contagious. When you are happy, your child will be free to feel merry, too.

Three-year-olds struggle with growing from dependence to independence. In infancy, your baby was completely dependent on you, but now she must learn to be independent. Assist her independence by encouraging her in every way. If children do not achieve emotional independence, they cannot become all that they can be as adults. Dressing up in grown-up clothes is one way children practice being individuals. If your preschooler shows an interest in playing dress-up, provide adult-sized clothes, hats, or easy-to-put-on props for dramatic play.

Resilience is important to your child's good mental health. How can you teach her to resolve some of her own problems? Do not rush in to rescue her. Do not explain how to do everything. Let your child discover how things work on her own.

To flourish, preschoolers need a balance between the familiar and the unfamiliar. Play games that he already knows, and teach him new games. Go to old, familiar places, and visit new, exciting spots. Routines offer three-year-olds a sense of security while new experiences challenge them to expand their social and emotional skills. Use some of the games in this chapter to stimulate your three-year-old's social and emotional growth.

Social/Emotional Milestones: Three Years

◆ Will begin learning how to cooperate
◆ Will begin learning how to share
◆ Will begin learning how to take turns
◆ Will begin learning how to postpone gratification
◆ Will play pretend games
◆ Will begin to understand the difference between "real" and "make-believe"
◆ May develop imaginary friends
◆ Will begin to dress and undress herself
◆ May be fearful of unfamiliar objects and think they are "monsters"
◆ Will begin learning how to relax
◆ May begin to develop empathy for other children

© Instructional Fair • TS Denison

 General Tips

Celebrate the good things about your preschooler. Make a list and hang it on the refrigerator door or somewhere else where everyone can see it. In the presence of your child, read the list to family and friends. Make up songs about his new accomplishments. When praising him:

◆ Express delight in behavior you wish to see repeated.

◆ Ignore behavior you want to see discontinued.

◆ Notice his progress as well as his achievements.

◆ Keep your encouragements specific.

◆ Acknowledge everything positive.

◆ Encourage him to use new skills again and again.

Do not see upsets with your child as part of an unescapable parenting pattern. See each upset as an isolated instance; things will go better next time. Resist the temptation to view negative events as part of a never-ending cycle. Learn from your mistakes, then go on to do things differently the next time.

In China, the word "crisis" has two symbols. One symbol means "danger" and the other one means "opportunity." Adopt this Chinese view when parenting. See each crisis as an opportunity to learn. Remember, a good sense of humor will make your struggle as a parent more enjoyable. When you can see something amusing in stressful situations, you are being a good role model for your child. Take time each day to laugh and enjoy life.

Social/Emotional Development **Three-Year-Old**

Let's Cooperate

I love you well, my little brother,
And you are fond of me.
Let us be kind to one another,
As brothers ought to be. . .
—Traditional Rhyme

Overture

Watch, and you will see that your three-year-old is much less selfish than he was at age two. He may now be able to play with other children and interact instead of playing alongside of them. As he develops he will become more aware of and sensitive to the feelings of his friends. Gradually he will stop competing and learn to cooperate with peers.

Performance

Play: To help your three-year-old learn how to cooperate, arrange activities that require your child to cooperate with you in order to complete a task.

What you will need: Coloring book, three crayons (red, blue, yellow)

How to play: Pick one page that you and your child will color together. Work with just the three crayons on the same page. Often ask if you can use the crayon that your child is using, and trade him for one of the other two colors. The small work space on the page will require cooperation on your child's part.

Finale

Baking biscuits is a good kitchen activity that you can use to teach your child cooperation. Have him stir the mix as you pour in the liquid and eggs. Using two large wooden spoons to stir the batter at the same time is good cooperation practice. Kneading the dough on a floored board can be done by four hands instead of just two. Use two round cookie cutters to cut out the biscuits. Take turns placing the biscuits on a baking sheet. When it is time to clean up in the kitchen, teach your child that cooperating—two people sharing the task—gets it done twice as quickly.

Encore

Dressing and undressing your child is another good time to practice cooperation. Ask your child to cooperate in the process.

Examples:

- ◆ Take off your shoes, and I will take off your socks.
- ◆ Push your foot into this boot while I push it on.
- ◆ Put on your pajama tops, then I will help you put on the bottoms.

Another task that can be used to teach your child about cooperation is undressing and dressing a doll. Ask your child to take off some of the clothes while you are removing another part of the clothing. Take turns and cooperate to remove the clothes. Then redress the doll working together at the same time. Perhaps your child will put the clothes on the top part of the doll while you put the clothes on the bottom half of the doll.

 © Instructional Fair • TS Denison

Sharing

. . . You shall learn to play with me,
And learn to use my toys;
And then I think that we shall be
Two happy little boys.
     —Traditional Rhyme

Overture

Watch your three-year-old at play with other children, and you may notice that she begins to develop friendships with certain children. As she learns to value certain children, she will begin to realize that she too has qualities that make her a desirable friend. Social skills such as sharing must be learned while interacting with others.

Performance

Play: Give your child an opportunity to learn how to share by coloring with only one crayon.

What you will need: Large circle drawn on paper, one crayon

How to play: Tell your child that the two of you have to color the circle. Color for awhile then give her the crayon to use for about twenty seconds. Then ask her to let you have a turn. Every few seconds, shuffle the crayon back and forth. Besides sharing, your child will be practicing taking turns. Congratulate yourselves when the circle is colored.

Finale

Use a small chalkboard and one piece of chalk to draw a picture with your child. Sharing the small space and the one writing instrument may be a bit frustrating for your child. If sharing seems to be extremely challenging for your child, practice these kinds of tasks for very short periods of time, but do not stop practicing.

Encore

Provide practice for sharing by playing with only one toy.
Examples:
- While she is playing with her favorite doll, ask to hold it for a few seconds.
- For a snack, provide only one cookie. Ask your child to share it with you. If she does not want to do this, try again on another day.
- Share a small glass of juice.
- Go to the park and buy a small bag of popcorn or peanuts and share them.
- Take a walk after dark and share a flashlight.
- Share a magnifying glass to look at bugs.

Bake Cookies

Pat-a-cake, pat-a-cake, baker's man!
Make me a cake as fast as you can: . . .
—Traditional Rhyme

Overture

Taking turns is sharing at an advanced level—a way of making sure that sharing is on an equal basis. Watch your child when he is asked to share a toy. Does he see it as a challenge?

Performance

Play: To encourage your three-year-old to take turns, bake cookies together.

What you will need: Large bowl, large wooden spoon or mixing spoon, cookie recipe and necessary ingredients or commercially prepared cookie dough, baking sheets

How to play: Prepare the cookie dough as directed on the recipe. Take turns stirring the batter with the wooden spoon. Each time you take a turn, talk about sharing and cooperating. When your child has his turn stirring, tell him how nice it is that he is willing to take turns. After a minute, ask him to let you have a turn. Repeat this process several times. When the cookie dough is ready, show him how to spoon the dough on the baking sheets. Then take turns forming the cookies. Bake as directed on the recipe or package. When the cookies are cool, enjoy your treats.

Finale

Many craft projects can be done as a team and require taking turns. Making a paper chain can be a project used to teach taking turns.

◆ Using only one pair of scissors, take turns cutting small strips of paper.
◆ Use only one glue stick and take turns gluing the rings to link them together.
◆ Take turns holding the ends of the paper until they dry and stick together permanently.

Encore

When you are teaching your child about taking turns, point out who had the last turn. For example: "It is my turn to turn the page because you turned the page last time." While playing games, encourage taking turns.

The great thing about taking turns is that your child knows that when it is his turn you have time to watch him because you are not performing the task. When two people are working at the same time, no one is watching the other person. By taking turns, your child is assured that half of the time you are focused on what he is doing instead of the task at hand.

       © Instructional Fair • TS Denison

In One Minute

Hickory, dickory, dock.
The mouse ran up the clock.
The clock struck one,
And down he run.
Hickory, dickory, dock.
—Traditional Rhyme

Overture

Watch a three-year-old, and you will see impatience working overtime. Although it is one of the most difficult skills a preschooler can learn, postponing gratification is paramount to becoming a happy, healthy child and adult.

Performance

Play: To help your three-year-old learn how to postpone gratification, play "In One Minute."

What you will need: Provide small treats that are appropriate for your child. It just has to be something she likes very much.

How to play: Place one treat on the table where your child can see it. Tell her she has a choice. She can eat it now or wait for one minute and get two instead of just one. Let her choose. Play the game only one time each day. If she eats the treat immediately, do not under any circumstances let her have another one until you are ready to present the game again on another day.

Finale

To reinforce patience, at least once a day, when your child asks you for something, tell her to wait for one to three minutes. Set a timer. Tell her when the timer goes off, she can have whatever it is for which she has asked. Practicing how to wait each day will help her establish an important life skill—patience.

Encore

One way to teach your child to postpone gratification is to set a good example. If she sees that you can wait for things you want, she will learn to do the same. Some ways to set an example of being patient include:

◆ Taking a few seconds each day to be still. Demonstrate sitting quietly without activity. Ask your child to not interrupt you during those few minutes. Watching you in a totally nonactive period of time will be setting a good example.

◆ Having a quiet time before meals. When everyone is seated at the table, take time for silence. Spending a minute or two at the table before beginning to eat is a way of demonstrating to your child that each family member has the patience to wait before beginning to eat.

◆ Having a quiet silent time before a bedtime story. Stopping all activity is difficult for three-year-olds. Providing time when your child is required to be still will give her a chance to practice this difficult skill.

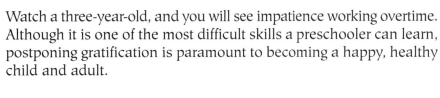

Let's Pretend

Here we come gathering acorns and hay,
Acorns and hay, acorns and hay.
Here we come gathering acorns and hay,
On a warm and sunny day.

Overture

Pretending is a three-year-old's way of dealing with a wide range of emotions. Love, independence, anger, anxiety, and fear are just a few of the emotions with which children deal in fantasy play. Watch your child at play; you will see various emotions incorporated into the games.

Performance

Play: Allow your three-year-old lots of opportunity for pretending. Encourage his imagination and creativity by playing pretend games with him.

What you will need: No special equipment is needed to pretend.

How to play: As you recite the rhyme, pretend to gather nuts and put them in an imaginary basket. Then recite the rhyme again and pretend to gather armloads of hay and pile the hay on an imaginary wagon. For additional miming fun, recite varied versions of the rhyme including:

◆ Here we come gathering berries and nuts, . . . on a hot summer day.
◆ Here we come gathering seashells and starfish, . . . on a sand-covered beach.
◆ Here we come picking pretty flowers, . . . on a bright spring day.
◆ Here we come gathering sticks and stones, . . . in a grass-covered woods.
◆ Here we are eating ice cream and cake, . . . at a birthday party.
◆ Here we come picking apples and plums, . . . in a big orchard.
◆ Here we are throwing snowballs, . . . on a cold winter day.

Finale

Miming is a good way to teach your child to pretend. Mime some of the following and invite your child to guess what you are pretending.

◆ Eating a sour pickle   ◆ Decorating a cake
◆ Flying   ◆ Riding a horse
◆ Riding a surfboard   ◆ Driving a car
◆ Flying a kite   ◆ Juggling

Encore

Ask your three-year-old to pretend to do things that he does every day including:

◆ Combing his hair   ◆ Getting dressed
◆ Brushing his teeth   ◆ Washing his face

 © Instructional Fair • TS Denison

Real or Make-Believe?

Hey diddle, diddle, the cat and the fiddle,
The cow jumped over the moon.
The little dog laughed to see such sport,
And the dish ran away with the spoon.
—Traditional Rhyme

Overture

Most three-year-olds cannot distinguish between fantasy and reality. Watch your child playing, and you will see her moving back and forth between fantasy and reality. Sometimes her make-believe games will feel so real to her that she will not realize where the game ends and reality begins. From time to time, join in your child's fantasy play.

Performance

Play: To help your three-year-old understand the difference between real and make-believe, as you read stories and look at picture books, ask questions.

What you will need: Nursery rhyme books with pictures

How to play: Read a rhyme or story. Ask questions about the rhymes.

Examples:
◆ "Hey Diddle, Diddle"—Can a cow jump over the moon?
◆ "Cinderella"—Can a pumpkin be turned into a carriage?
◆ "The Three Bears"—Do bears live in houses?
◆ "Jack and the Beanstalk"—Do giants really live in the clouds?

When your child knows something cannot really happen, it is a perfect time to talk about "make-believe."

Finale

On other occasions when you are looking at books and magazines, point to objects and ask her if they are real or make-believe.

Encore

The concept of real versus make-believe is very complicated. At this stage of development, your child should just be introduced to the subject; she does not need to have total comprehension. For example, Cinderella is make-believe but a representation of the make-believe character can be seen dancing on the screen. A lion is real but not often, if ever, seen by the child. Because one is a person and the other is something your child never sees, she might think Cinderella is real and lions are make-believe. When an object exists somewhere other than where the child is, sometimes that thing may seem make-believe. Visiting a zoo to see a lion will make it clear that lions are real. Providing a wide range of exploration in the world will help your child separate reality from fantasy.

Imaginary Friends

Respect the child. . . . Trespass not on his solitude.
—Ralph Waldo Emerson

Overture ....

Many three-year-olds develop imaginary friends. Often the imaginary friends can perform miracles and do bad things without being punished. If your child shares with you about an imaginary friend, he may talk about the friend as if he is real. Listen, but do not ask questions about the imaginary friend.

Performance ....

Play: To help your three-year-old express his imagination, respect the private nature of his fantasy play.

What you will need: No special equipment is necessary for this activity.

How to play: The best way to respect your child's imaginary friend is to not get involved in the fantasy. If you invade his privacy by asking about the friend, you will transport him from a place of make-believe to reality. His imaginary friend will disappear as soon as you begin real life conversations. If your child wants to have a conversation about his imaginary friend, listen, but do not question him about his friend. Let him say what he wants to share. If you invade his privacy by asking about the friend, the magic will disappear.

Finale ....

Encourage your child's make-believe play in different ways, such as:
- ◆ Sometimes pretending with him
- ◆ Reading make-believe stories to him
- ◆ Watching videos and movies together about make-believe characters

Encore ....

Give your child ideas for make-believe games.
- ◆ Pretend to be fairy tale characters (Peter Pan, Snow White)
- ◆ Pretend to be adults that the child knows (Father, Grandmother)
- ◆ Pretend to be in interesting places (zoo, circus, fair)
- ◆ Pretend to be grown-ups with different occupations (doctor, teacher, race car driver, astronaut, police officer, firefighter, dentist)
- ◆ Pretend to be performing household jobs (cooking, cleaning)
- ◆ Pretend to be doing yard jobs (raking, digging, mowing the lawn)
- ◆ Pretend to be doing grown-up tasks (driving a car)

 © Instructional Fair • TS Denison

Dress Up

Little Miss Lily, you're dreadfully silly
To wear such a very long skirt.
If you take my advice, you would hold it up nice
And not let it trail in the dirt.
——Traditional Rhyme

Overture

Self-care is a skill that will give your three-year-old much pride of accomplishment. Getting dressed on her own is one of the first self-care skills she will master. Giving her choices about her clothing will help her celebrate her independence and creativity.

Performance

Play: To reinforce your three-year-old's dressing skills, provide a box of adult-sized dress-up clothes for her to use as costumes.

What you will need: If possible, provide a full-length mirror for your child to use during dress-up sessions. In a large box place a variety of men's and women's clothing including:

◆ Shoes, boots, slippers
◆ Scarves, belts, capes
◆ Dresses, shirts
◆ Jackets, sweaters, coats
◆ Raincoat, mittens, gloves
◆ Sunglasses, hats, caps, bonnets
◆ Props such as a magic wand

How to play: Engage in dressing up and playing with your child, but also encourage her to dress up and play on her own. Part of the joy of fantasy is being able to control the imaginary happenings; if you are always there, it will limit her imaginary play.

Finale

Some ethnic clothing in the dress-up box will enrich your child's play.
Examples:
◆ Hawaiian shirt and grass skirt
◆ Dashiki
◆ Sari

Encore

Take photographs of your child in a variety of dress-up clothes. Put each photograph on a page in a spiral bound notebook. Ask your child to tell you about each photograph and record her thoughts about each outfit. Look at the photographs and read the book to your child.

The Monster Mash

When on the road to Thebes,
Oedipus met the Sphinx,
who asked him her riddle,
his answer was: Man.
This simple word destroyed the monster.
—George Seferis

Overture

Watch, and you will notice that your three-year-old may be fearful of unfamiliar objects and think they are "monsters." Talking about "monsters" and pretending to be a monster helps most three-year-olds deal with fears.

Performance

Play: To help your child deal with his fears, do "The Monster Mash."
What you will need: Marching music
How to play: The object of the dance is to pretend to be monsters. Put on the music and march around. Stomp. Pound feet on the floor. Make weird sounds. Let your child use his imagination and take the lead.

Finale

Another good way to deal with your three-year-old's fears is to have him draw pictures of "monsters." Ask him questions about the pictures.

◆ What color are "monsters?"
◆ What games do "monsters" play?
◆ Do "mommy monsters" have baby monsters?
◆ What do "monsters" eat?

Encore

There are things you can do to help lower your child's level of anxiety about unfamiliar things including:

◆ If he is afraid of the dark, provide a nightlight in his room.
◆ Do not allow him to watch scary television shows or movies.
◆ Deal with each fear as it comes up.
◆ Validate his concerns by listening to his fears.
◆ Avoid situations that will bring up anxieties.
◆ Reassure him when he is frightened or upset.
◆ Do not belittle or make fun of his fears.

© Instructional Fair • TS Denison

Breathe and Blow

Sweet and low, sweet and low,
Wind of the western sea,
Low, low, breathe and blow,
Wind of the western sea!
—Alfred Lord Tennyson

Overture

Watch your child playing, and you will see that playing is her work. Most three-year-olds never stop; they go from early morning until they drop off to sleep at night. You will not have to teach her how to play, but you may have to teach her how to take a break from play to relax.

Performance

Play: To help your three-year-old learn how to relax, teach her how to breathe deeply.
What you will need: Balloon
How to play: Show your child the balloon before your blow it up. Have her watch you inflate it. Then let go of the pinched end and let the air out of the balloon very slowly. Watch it deflate. After your child has watched this demonstration, pretend to be balloons. Begin by sitting on the floor. Take a long deep breath. Imagine that you are a balloon getting bigger and bigger until completely full. Then hold the breath for a few seconds. Exhale very slowly. Pretend that the air being inhaled is inflating the body. Each time you breathe out, pretend to be a deflating balloon. Practice until your child can inhale very deep breaths, hold, and exhale slowly.

Finale

Use deep breathing to have your child pretend:
- She is a sailboat being driven across the water with each breath.
- She is a flower growing and blooming.
- She is the wind with each exhale.
- She is a cloud being driven by each breath.

Encore

On other occasions, make up stories about sleepy people. Take turns "yawning" when appropriate for the story line. Another technique is to count slowly to six to help your child relax or fall asleep. Follow these four easy steps:
- Count slowly to six while she inhales a deep breath.
- Count slowly to six while she holds her breath.
- Count slowly to six as she exhales.
- Count slowly to six before the next breath.

Don't Cry, Baby

Cry, baby, cry. . . .

Overture

At three-years-old, children sometimes begin to develop empathy for others. Watch when your child sees another child crying; he may become distressed or even want to help the other child.

Performance

Play: To encourage your three-year-old to have empathy for others, play "Don't Cry, Baby."
What you will need: Baby doll, baby blanket, child-sized rocking chair or chair
How to play: Invite your child to play house. Tell him the doll is the baby. Pretend to be the doll crying. Say something like this, "Oh, I hear the baby crying." Pick up the doll. Wrap it in a little blanket. Tell the doll, "Don't cry, baby." Then encourage your child to rock the dolly to sleep. Talk in whispers. You can find out about your child's feelings by asking questions including:
- ◆ Why do you think the baby is crying?
- ◆ What makes the baby happy?
- ◆ What makes the baby feel safe?
- ◆ What makes the baby afraid?
- ◆ What makes the baby laugh?

Pretend to put the baby down for a nap. In a few minutes, pretend to be the baby crying again. Repeat the comforting steps.

Finale

You can encourage your child's feelings of empathy by discussing how others feel. When watching a movie, ask about the different feelings the characters may be experiencing:
- ◆ How do you think the child feels?
- ◆ What do you think made him feel this way?
- ◆ What do you think would make him feel better?
- ◆ Have you ever felt the same way?
- ◆ What causes you to feel this way?
- ◆ What helps you feel better?

Encore

One way to teach empathy for others is to have your child explore his own feelings. Use a hand mirror to have your child explore different feelings. After hearing each question, have him show you an appropriate face.
- ◆ How would it feel to have your favorite toy broken?
- ◆ How would it feel to be locked out of the house?
- ◆ How would it feel to get lost in the mall?
- ◆ How would it feel to get a new toy?
- ◆ How would it feel to drop your favorite ice cream on the ground?
- ◆ How would it feel to hear that your father (uncle, aunt, grandparent, etc.) thinks you are the smartest kid in the whole world?

© Instructional Fair • TS Denison

Keeping Track

Milestone	Date	Comments
Can cooperate with playmates		
Can share with others		
Can take turns		
Can postpone gratification		
Can play pretend games		
Understands the difference between real and make-believe		
Has an imaginary friend		
Can dress and undress self		
May be fearful of the unfamiliar		
Can relax and breathe deeply		
Has empathy for other children		

Thinkercizes

Cognitive Development

Contemplate

A child's learning is greatly dependent on his feelings of self-importance. When you verbally praise your preschooler, he feels your love and is given the space to grow, feel worthy, and learn to love himself. When he learns self-worth, he will have the courage to try new things thus accelerating his learning. Play stimulates the three-year-old's cognitive and creative development.

Most three-year-olds spend their days asking questions. Their play is experimental and they especially like exploring new places. They like to build large constructions with boxes, boards, blankets, etc. Forts, playhouses, and tents provide secret, private places for fantasy. Use the learning games in this chapter to boast your child's cognitive skills.

Cognitive Milestones: Three Years

◆ Will learn how to count to three or even five
◆ Will learn the names of the primary colors: red, yellow, and blue
◆ Will begin to understand the time concepts "day" and "night"
◆ Will learn how to follow a series of commands
◆ Will be able to retell a short, repetitive story
◆ Will learn to use tools such as hammer and nails
◆ Will know the names of most body parts: knees, elbows, hips, ankles, etc.
◆ Will be able to sort by size (small, medium, and large)
◆ Will be able to sort by shape (squares, circles, and triangles)
◆ Will be able to sort primary colors (red, blue, and yellow)
◆ Will be able to name similar attributes of size, shape, and color
◆ Will understand the concept "now" and "later"
◆ Will understand the concept of humor and know when you are joking
◆ Will learn about "wishes"
◆ Will learn from new experiences

© Instructional Fair • TS Denison

 ## General Tips

Pretending is an excellent way for preschoolers to practice creativity. Developing a good imagination during childhood is vital for emotional growth and becoming a happy child and productive adult. When a child sees an adult pretending and playing, she is more free to pretend and express her imagination, too. Encourage verbalization, creativity, and imagination by playing "What If" games.

Examples:

- ◆ What if root beer came out of the faucet instead of water?
- ◆ What if it snowed cotton instead of snow?
- ◆ What if cookies grew on trees instead of leaves?
- ◆ What if cats quacked instead of purred?
- ◆ What if you had one wish that would come true?
- ◆ What if you could fly by flapping your arms?
- ◆ What if you could walk on the ceiling?
- ◆ What if you were invisible?
- ◆ What if animals could speak?
- ◆ What if you could breathe underwater and swim like a fish?
- ◆ What if you had eyes in the back of your head?

Preschoolers cannot always verbalize their thoughts, and the answers to the "What If" questions are not important. The important thing is to teach your child how to ask interesting questions and think in wild and fanciful ways. Playing is a great way to express feelings and learn at the same time. Playing is your child's work. Every way your child plays is okay.

Reading to your preschooler will stimulate her cognitive skills. Book about the five senses are especially stimulating for cognitive learning. Some examples include:

- ◆ *Brown Bear, Brown Bear, What Do You See?* by Bill Martin, Jr. (Henry Holt, 1996)
- ◆ *The Eye Book* by Dr. Seuss (Random House, 1999)
- ◆ *The Ear Book* by Al Perkins (Random House, 1968)
- ◆ *How Do Your Senses Work? (Flip Flaps Series)* by Judy Tatchell (EDC Publications, 1998)
- ◆ *I Smell Honey* by Andrea and Brian Pinkney (Red Wagon, 1997)
- ◆ *Nicky's Noisy Night (Lift the Flap Books)* by Harriet Ziefert (Viking Press, 1986)
- ◆ *The Nose Book* by Al Perkins (Random House, 1989)
- ◆ *A Peekaboo Book with Flaps and a Mirror! Where Is Your Nose?* by Trisha Lee Shappie (Cartwheel Books, 1997)
- ◆ *Polar Bear, Polar Bear, What Do You Hear?* by Bill Martin, Jr. (Henry Holt, 1991)

Run to the Tree

One, two, three, run to the tree.
One, two, three, run back to me.

Overture ....

For most three-year-olds, the number three is a favorite number. Many three-year-olds can count to three and recognize three objects as "three" without counting each one.

Performance ....

Play: To give your preschooler an opportunity to learn how to count to three, play "Run to the Tree."
What you will need: Area with a large tree
How to play: As you show the appropriate number of fingers, say the rhyme.

> One, (*Show one finger.*)
> Two, (*Show two fingers.*)
> Three, (*Show three fingers.*)
> Run to the tree. (*Child runs to the tree, tags it, and stops there.*)
> One, (*Show one finger.*)
> Two, (*Show two fingers.*)
> Three, (*Show three fingers.*)
> Run back to me. (*Child runs back to you. Grab him up and give him a hug.*)

Reverse the game and have your preschooler say the rhyme, show the appropriate number of fingers, and send you racing off to the tree.

Finale ....

To reinforce counting, assemble three teddy bears or other stuffed animals. Place one on the table, and help your preschooler count it. "One." Then put another bear on the table. Count the bears. "One, two." Then put the third bear on the table. Count all three. Count with your child, and then let him count the bears alone. See if he can name the number of bears without counting. Does he know three things without counting each one? Does he recognize two things without counting first? Practice counting to three. If appropriate, gather a collection of four or five stuffed animals or toys for your child to count.

Encore ....

On other occasions, when you and your child are out and about and you see pairs of things or things in groups of three, say something like this: "Look at the two kittens," or "Do you see those three dogs?" If your child easily recognizes groups of three, start talking about groups of four. Later, work up to groups of five.

© Instructional Fair • TS Denison

Paper Collages

Red, yellow, or blue?
It's all up to you.
Red, yellow, or blue?
Take your pick and glue.

Overture

At three years of age, most children have a favorite color. Red is the favorite color of many preschoolers. Observe your child's choices, and you will discover which is her favorite color.

Performance

Play: To give your preschooler an opportunity to learn the names of the primary colors (red, yellow, and blue) make tricolor paper collages.

What you will need: Red, yellow, and blue sheets of construction paper, large sheet of heavy paper or light cardboard, glue stick

How to play: Cut a circle, square, and triangle from each color of construction paper. Show your child how to place some of the colorful shapes on the paper in a pleasing way. Overlap and balance the colors and shapes. Then remove them, and let your child create a collage of paper shapes. As she places each paper cutout on the paper, name the color and shape. "You are putting the red circle on now" or "I like that yellow square." Arrange and rearrange until she gets a design that she likes. Then help her use the glue stick to attach each colorful shape in its place. Set the collage aside to dry.

Finale

Use the tricolor paper collage to talk about colors and shapes. Ask her to point to a particular color or shape, such as:

- A red (blue, yellow) shape
- The yellow circle (square, triangle)
- The blue shape that is touching a red circle

Encore

On another occasion, go on a primary color scavenger hunt. Give your preschooler a grocery-sized bag with the word "red" written in red crayon on the side of the bag. Look around the house for things that are red. Put them in the bag. Go through dresser drawers, and look for a pair of red socks, mittens, or scarves. Go outside to look for red things to put in the bag. Flip through old magazines and look for pictures of things that are red. Put those in the bag, too. When your hunt is complete, take the bag to a table. Pour out the contents. Talk about each item. How many can your child name? Include the color of each object when discussing it. On another day go on a "blue" or "yellow" scavenger hunt.

Hello, Sun—Good Night, Moon

Hello, Sun—good night, Moon.
Wake me up when it is light.
Tuck me in when it is night.

Overture

For most three-year-olds, "night" means bedtime. Watch your child at bedtime. Is he afraid he will miss out on something while he is sleeping? Winding down at bedtime can be a slow process. Sometimes it helps to begin with a warm bath and follow up with a quiet song or story. Whatever the ritual, following it daily will make bedtime easier for both of you.

Performance

Play: To help your preschooler begin to understand the concepts of "day" and "night," play "Hello, Sun—Good Night, Moon."
What you will need: No special equipment is needed for this activity.
How to play: Every day, make it a ritual to say "good morning" to the sun and "good night" to the moon. Taking some quiet time at the beginning and end of each day can become a lifelong act of appreciation for your child.

Finale

Reinforce night and day by making two collages—one on black construction paper and one on white paper. You will need old magazines, scissors, and a glue stick. Cut out pictures of people, animals, buildings, etc. Use the glue stick to glue the pictures on the sheets of black and white paper. Talk about the black paper being a nighttime picture and the white paper being a daytime picture.

Encore

Another good way to teach your preschooler about time is to divide the day into mealtimes. Discuss that you eat breakfast in the morning, lunch in the middle of the day, and dinner at night. When you go places, talk about whether it is daytime or nighttime. When you put your child to bed at night, tell him "I will see you tomorrow." Bedtime stories that teach about day and night include:

◆ *Goodnight, Moon* by Margaret Wise Brown (HarperCollins, 1991)
◆ *A Snowy Day* by Ezra Jack Keats (Viking Press, 1962)

© Instructional Fair • TS Denison

Toy Parade

Smiling girls, rosy boys,
Come and buy my little toys;
Monkeys made of gingerbread,
And sugar horses painted red.
—Traditional Rhyme

Overture

Watch your child while you are explaining something. If she is listening, you will be able to tell by her facial expression and body language that she is concentrating and comprehending. If she is not paying attention, she probably will not understand what you want her to do.

Performance

Play: To teach your preschooler how to follow a series of commands, play "Toy Parade."

What you will need: A variety of stuffed animals or toys (at least ten different ones), big bag or box

How to play: Sit on the floor with the toys between you and your child. Put three of the stuffed animals in a row as if they are parading. Talk about the order of the animals. "Look at the pig 'first' in the parade. The teddy bear is 'last' in the parade. What is in the middle?" Then put the animals back in the box or bag. Ask your child to make a parade of three animals that you name. Then when the parade of animals is made, give two-part commands such as:

- ◆ Put the pig "first" and the teddy bear "last" in the parade.
- ◆ Put the pig "in the middle" and the teddy bear "first" in the parade.
- ◆ Put the lion "last" and the teddy bear "in the middle" of the parade.

Repeat using three different animals. Each time, tell your child two things to do to rearrange the parade of three animals. If this is too difficult, just give one command at a time, and eventually work up to two commands.

Finale

Use paper cutouts to play the same game. Cut out red, blue, and yellow circles, triangles, and squares. You will have nine cutouts all together. Place three cutouts in a row. Then give your child a series of three commands. Repeat the instructions as many times as your child needs to hear them.

- ◆ Put the red square "first." Put the yellow triangle "in the middle." Put the blue square "last."
- ◆ Put the yellow triangle "first," followed by the red square, and put the blue square "last."

Your child can use either the color or shape clue when working with the three cutouts.

Encore

Use a series of three commands to have your child complete self-care tasks.
Examples:

- ◆ Take off your shoes and socks, put them in your room, and then get the book you want me to read to you.
- ◆ Pick up your toys, bring a book to me, and then climb into my lap.
- ◆ Eat your sandwich, finish your milk, and then wash your face.

Finish the Rhyme

Little boy blue, come blow your horn;
The sheep's in the meadow, the cow's in the corn.
Where's the little boy that looks after the sheep?
He's under the haystack, fast asleep.
Will you wake him? No, not I;
For if I do, he'll be sure to cry.
                                      —Traditional Rhyme

Overture

Three-year-olds often memorize short stories and rhymes. Listen as you read a story that your child knows. If you pause, he may say the next word. When you are reading remember the two magical words: "Pause" and "Applause." Pause to give your child an opportunity to give a word or line and applaud every effort he makes to share in the telling of the story.

Performance

Play: To help your preschooler learn how to remember nursery rhymes, play "Finish the Line."
What you will need: Picture books with simple nursery rhymes.
How to play: Choose nursery rhymes with rhyming words which give the child a clue to the ending. Recite the rhyme. When you come to the last word, pause and let your child fill in the missing word. Wait, and if he cannot provide the word, then say it. Repeat the process until he is familiar with the rhyme and can say the last word of each line.

Little boy blue, come blow your _____ (horn);
The sheep's in the meadow, the cow's in the _____ (corn).
Where's the little boy that looks after the _____ (sheep)?
He's under the haystack, fast _____ (asleep).
Will you wake him? No, not _____ (I);
For if I do, he'll be sure to _____ (cry).

Finale

Use the rhyme game with other familiar nursery rhymes, too.

Mary had a little _____ (lamb)
With fleece as white as _____ (snow),
And everywhere that Mary _____ (went)
The lamb was sure to _____ (go).

Little Jack Horner sat in a _____ (corner),
Eating a Christmas pie. He put in his _____ (thumb),
And pulled out a plum, and said, "What a good boy am _____ (I)"!

Encore

Sing familiar tunes like "Happy Birthday" and "Twinkle, Twinkle, Little Star." Pause to let your child fill in the last word of a line. Most three-year-olds enjoy this kind of game.

          © Instructional Fair • TS Denison

Workbench

Tit, tat, toe, my first go.
Three jolly butcher boys all in a row.
Stick one up, stick one down,
Stick one on the old man's crown.
—Traditional Rhyme

Overture ....

Most three-year-olds enjoy using a hammer and nails. Watch your child hammering a nail into a board, and you will see intense concentration.

Performance ....

Play: To help your preschooler learn how to use tools such as a hammer and nails, provide a place for her to practice hammering nails.

What you will need: Workbench, nails with large heads, lightweight hammer with a large head

How to play: Drive some nails into the board about halfway so they are secure. Show your child how to hold the hammer at the end of the handle and hit a nail directly on the head. Stay with your child as she learns how to hammer the nails. Be sure to teach her to hold her other hand safely away from the workbench.

Finale ....

For an additional activity using the workbench, after you have driven in some nails halfway, give your child a ball of yarn. Tie one end of the yarn to the base of one of the nails. Wrapping the yarn around individual nails, help your child create a random design with the yarn. Later the yarn can be removed and wrapped in a different design.

Encore ....

Three-year-olds enjoy working with wood. As assisted play, have your child create wood sculptures. Use wood glue to attach pieces of wood together in random ways. If interested, encourage your child to collect natural objects like twigs, pinecones, feathers, shells, moss, etc. Using school glue, let your child glue the objects to a big piece of bark.

Touch Together

Head and shoulders, knees and toes, knees and toes.
Head and shoulders, knees and toes, knees and toes.
Eyes and ears and mouth and nose,
Head and shoulders, knees and toes, knees and toes.
—Traditional Song

Overture

For awhile now, your three-year-old has probably known the names for basic body parts like head, hands, arms, fingers, etc. However, learning the more obscure parts like elbow, ankle, wrist, throat, heel, etc. may take longer to learn.

Performance

Play: To help your preschooler learn to name all the parts of the body, play "Touch Together."
What you will need: No special equipment is needed to play this game.
How to play: Seated on the floor in front of your child, give verbal directions and provide body language to guide your child in using a particular part of his body to touch the same part of your body. Examples:

- ◆ Touch my elbows with your elbows.
- ◆ Touch our wrists together.
- ◆ Touch the palms of our hands together.
- ◆ Touch your hip to my hip.
- ◆ Touch our backs together.
- ◆ Touch all of our fingertips together.
- ◆ Touch the soles of our feet together.

Give directions for touching different body parts together—the sillier the better. Examples:

- ◆ Touch my knee with your toes.
- ◆ Touch my cheek with your ear.
- ◆ Put the soles of your feet in the palms of my hands.
- ◆ Touch my ankles with your thumbs.
- ◆ Touch my forehead with your knuckles.

Finale

To reinforce verbal skills, touch parts of your body together, and have your child tell you what is touching. You ask, "What is touching?"
Examples:

- ◆ Touch your hand to one elbow. (Child says, "hand and elbow.")
- ◆ Touch your elbows to your knees.
- ◆ Touch your thumb (fingers, wrist) to your lips.
- ◆ Touch one heel (ankle, wrist, palm) to your toes.
- ◆ Touch your tongue to your lips.
- ◆ Touch your thumb to your ear (eyebrow, nose, chin, cheek, neck).

Encore

On other occasions, touch identical body parts and move to music. Examples: palms of hands, fingertips, toes, heels, etc. Sitting or standing, match a body part that you or your child names, then try to move to music without separating the connection.

        © Instructional Fair • TS Denison

Little or Big?

Little maid, little maid, whither goest thou?
Down in the meadow to milk my cow.
—Traditional Rhyme

Overture

A child learns best when she is learning for herself and not to please her parents or others. The best way to help your child learn is to provide a variety of experiences and praise her every accomplishment.

Performance

Play: To help your child learn to sort by size, play "Little or Big?"
What you will need: Picture books or children's magazines
How to play: Sit with your child on your lap so she can see the pictures. Point to a picture and name it. For example, when looking at a picture of a cow, ask, "Are cows little or big?" Of course the picture of the cow might be little, so this game may be confusing at first. You will need to let her know you want to discuss the size of the object represented by the picture, not the picture, itself. One way to do this is to look at a picture of a car. Then go to the garage and look at an automobile. Say something like, "This is a picture of a big car. Cars are big."

Finale

When you feel that your child understands the concept of "little" and "big," play a game of sorting by size without using pictures. Name two objects and have your child tell you which one is "smaller" or which one is "bigger."
Examples:
◆ Which is smaller—car or candy bar?
◆ Which is bigger—house or quarter?
◆ Which is smaller—marshmallow or tree?
◆ Which is bigger—barn or mouse?
◆ Which is smaller—giraffe or spider?
◆ Which is bigger—ocean or seashell?

Encore

When you take a walk, name two things your child can see, and ask which one is "smaller" or which one is "bigger." Then when you get home, ask her about the size of the things again.

Sorting Jelly Beans

Red is cherry; blue is berry.
Yellow is lemon; come pick one.
Green is apple; have a sample.

Overture

When teaching a preschooler, it is important to watch and approve, but never push. A happy learner will learn more quickly and enjoy the process. Watch your child playing, and tell him how smart he is.

Performance

Play: To teach your child to sort by primary colors (red, yellow, blue) or secondary colors (green, purple, orange), play "Sorting Jelly Beans."
What you will need: Bag of gourmet jelly beans, clear plastic cups
How to play: Pour the jelly beans out on the table. Put a different color jelly bean in the bottom of each cup. Show your child how to put the same color of jelly beans into each container. Leave him to finish the sorting on his own.

Finale

After sorting the jelly beans, taste one of each color. Talk about the flavor of each jelly bean. Look in the kitchen for the foods that have the same flavor.
◆ Yellow jelly beans are lemon flavored. Do lemons taste like yellow jelly beans? How are they different?
◆ Taste a green apple jelly bean and an apple. How are they similar? How are they different?
◆ What flavor are the brown ones? Do brown jelly beans taste more like hot chocolate or chocolate ice cream?

Encore

On other occasions, talk about shades of different colors. Some blues are almost green. Some reds are almost pink or purple. Gather a variety of blue objects. Look at the different shades. On another day, gather a variety of red objects and do the same. Repeat with different colors. Your child might like to learn the name for light red (pink) or the color of bluish green (turquoise), etc.

© Instructional Fair • TS Denison

Shape Up!

Square, circle, or triangle?
Everything has a shape.

Overture

Three-year-olds enjoy looking for similarities and differences in the things they see around them. They automatically sort things in their minds. This sorting of objects is important to their language and cognitive development.

Performance

Play: To teach your child to sort by shape, such as squares, circles, or triangles, play "Shape Up!"

What you will need: Three large grocery bags, colorful paper cutout of each shape, glue stick

How to play: Fold down the top of each bag to make sturdy containers. Glue a shape to the side of each bag. Then with your child, look around the house for objects that are either round, square, or triangular. As you find the objects, have your child place them in the appropriate bag. Name the shapes over and over as you are playing.

Finale

When you are out and about, talk about the shapes of things.
- Take a hike around the neighborhood looking for round, square, or triangular shapes. Can you find a house with a roof that looks triangular?
- Look at the night sky, and see if you can find a round thing—a full moon.
- When you are shopping at a supermarket, encourage your child to look at the round fruit, square boxes, triangular designs on packages, and so on.

Encore

Talk about the shapes of things without viewing them:
- What shape are tires?
- What shape are some houses?
- What shape is a box?
- What shape is a doughnut?
- What shape is something with three sides?
- What shape is an orange?

Sorting by Attributes

Red, blue, yellow—all in a row,
Bend the bow—it's a rainbow.

Overture ....

Three-year-olds can think in abstract terms and reason. As they acquire language, they can sort things and spot similarities and differences. Watch to see if your child recognizes attributes such as size, shape, and color. Learning to sort by attributes will boost your child's thinking and reasoning skills.

Performance ....

Play: To help your child learn how to name similar attributes such as size, shape, and color, play "Sorting by Attributes."

What you will need: Paper shapes as follows, one of each:
- ◆ Large red, blue, yellow squares
- ◆ Large red, blue, yellow circles
- ◆ Large red, blue, yellow triangles
- ◆ Small red, blue, yellow squares
- ◆ Small red, blue, yellow circles
- ◆ Small red, blue, yellow triangles

How to play: Place two paper cutouts on the table, and ask if they are the same color? Size? Shape? Then place two other cutouts on the table and ask about each attribute again. Gather all of the cutouts in a pile, then place three shapes on the table and ask your child which one is a different shape or color or size than the other two.

Finale...

Place a cutout on the table. Ask your child to find a cutout that is the same color (shape, size). Discuss the two cutouts. How are they the same? How are they different?

Encore...

To advance the game, place two shapes on the table and ask your child to tell you how they are the same. For example: "They are both red." Then ask if they are the same size. If both are "big" and "red," say something like this, "They are the same color and the same size, but they are not the same shape."

  © Instructional Fair • TS Denison

Not Now—Later

Burnie bee, burnie bee,
Tell me when your wedding be?
If it be tomorrow day,
Take your wings and fly away.
—Traditional Rhyme

Overture

Concepts like "now" and "later," "yesterday" and "tomorrow," and others that deal with time are difficult for three-year-olds to grasp. Acting out "now" and "later" is a good way to engage your child in a personal way.

Performance

Activity: To help your child understand the concepts "now" and "later" and practice patience, play "Not Now—Later."

What you will need: No special equipment is needed to do this activity.

How to play: When your child asks to do something or indicates that she wants to do something, say, "Not now—later." Set the timer for one or two minutes. When the timer goes off, say, "Now it is later and you can do what you asked to do."

Finale

Use the terms "now" and "later" when describing your child's day.
- ◆ "Now" we are getting you dressed. "Later" I will take you to the park.
- ◆ "Now" your father is at work. "Later" he will come home for dinner.
- ◆ "Now" it is light outside. "Later" it will get dark.
- ◆ "Now" we are talking. "Later" you can play by yourself in your room.

Ask questions about time.
- ◆ When are we having lunch?
- ◆ When will we eat dinner?
- ◆ When will you take a nap?
- ◆ When will you take your bath?

Encore

Three-year-olds do not usually use the terms "today," "yesterday," and "tomorrow." When you feel it is appropriate for your child, introduce the concepts "today," "yesterday," and "tomorrow" by simply using them in your everyday conversations. Discuss things you did "yesterday" and things you are doing "today" or things you will do "tomorrow." For example:
- ◆ Yesterday, we went to the park. Do you remember feeding the ducks yesterday?
- ◆ Today, we are going to the supermarket. Do you want to go to the supermarket today?
- ◆ Tomorrow, Daddy will be home all day, and we will go for a walk tomorrow.

Just Joking

Dickery, dickery, dare,
The pig flew up in the air; . . .
—Traditional Rhyme

Overture

Listen to the way your three-year-old talks to adults, and you will have a good gauge of his developing self-confidence. Watch to see if he is friendly, talkative, and curious; these are good signs of positive self-esteem. With his new-found confidence will come experimentation. Three-year-olds grasp humor and usually enjoy joking with others.

Performance

Play: To help your three-year-old understand the concept of humor and know when you are joking, play "Just Joking."

What you will need: No special equipment is needed to play this game.

How to play: Make statements, and your child is to say if they are "true" or if you are "just joking."
- ◆ Today, I saw a pig flying in the sky.
- ◆ Yesterday, I took a bath.
- ◆ When you were a baby, I liked to sing songs to you.
- ◆ Tomorrow, I am going to paint the whole house blue.
- ◆ Dill pickles are sour like bananas.
- ◆ When I was a little girl, I was so small I lived in a matchbox.
- ◆ When Daddy was a little boy, he liked to ride his bike.

Finale

Share the Dr. Seuss book *And To Think I Saw It on Mulberry Street* (Random House 1989). Look at the pictures and find things that are real and things that are make-believe.

Encore

On other occasions, tell jokes to your child. Very simple jokes such as elephant jokes are sometimes enjoyed by three-year-olds. When you tell a joke, talk about what makes it funny.
- ◆ When an elephant takes a vacation to Hawaii, how much luggage does he need? (Just his trunk.)
- ◆ Why do elephants paint their toenails red? (So they can hide in the strawberry patches.)
- ◆ What time is it when an elephant sits on your fence? (Time to get a new fence.)
- ◆ What do you feed a large elephant? (Anything he wants.)
- ◆ How can you tell if an elephant has been in your refrigerator? (There are footprints in the butter.)
- ◆ How do you get five elephants into a compact car? (Two in the front seats and three in the back seat.)

© Instructional Fair • TS Denison

Star Light, Star Bright

Star light, star bright,
First star I see tonight.
I wish I may, I wish I might,
Have the wish I wish tonight.
　　　—Traditional Rhyme

Overture

For a three-year-old, believing in magic and making wishes is common place. One way to distinguish magic from wishes is to explain if we ask a person for something, it is a wish.

Performance

Play: To teach your three-year-old the difference between magic and wishes, play "Star Light, Star Bright."

What you will need: First evening star (Venus—the first "star" seen in the sky at night)

How to play: Go outside early in the evening. Venus (the planet) can usually be seen in the sky before dark. Teach your child the rhyme. Say it together. Make a wish. Then talk about what would have to happen for the wish to come true. Example: If your child wished for a tricycle, what would have to happen for the tricycle to become a reality? (Someone would have to go to a store, pick out the tricycle, pay for it, bring it home, and give it to the child.)

Finale

Discuss what steps must happen before other wishes can come true. Ask your child questions:
- ◆ If you make a wish and blow out the candles, and do not tell anyone, can Mom/Dad help you get your wish?
- ◆ If you wish for a new toy, who would you tell about your wish?
- ◆ If you wished you could grow tall overnight, could that happen? Would it help to tell someone about your wish?

Encore

On other occasions, explain that when your child wishes for something and tells someone the wish, that person may be able to make the wish come true. Also, help your child understand that wishing for something does not make it happen. For example, if your child is angry and wishes that another person would go away and never come back, and that person does move away or dies, she might think she caused it to happen. Let your child know that wishes are never magic.

Out and About!

Where have you been all the day, my boy, Willy?
Where have you been all the day, my boy, Willy? . . .
—Traditional Rhyme

Overture

Watch your three-year-old, and you will see that she is less fearful of new experiences than she was at age two. She will probably see brand-new experiences as adventurous and fun. Some of the activities that brought her comfort as a two-year-old will now seem boring to her.

Performance

Play: To encourage new experiences, take your three-year-old out on weekly or bimonthly adventures.
What you will need: Transportation and sometimes tickets
How to play: Before an outing, let your child help you choose a place to visit. Talk about it for at least one day before you leave on your adventure. Discuss what you and your child will need. Predict the things you will see. Ask questions that can be answered on the outing. The day of the outing, discuss appropriate clothes and shoes for the adventure. Let your child help decide what she will wear. Discuss the best time to leave for the outing. When you return home from the outing, talk and let her draw pictures about it.

Finale

Outings stimulate and inspire a preschooler's social, emotional, and cognitive growth. Set aside a day each week or every other week to take your preschooler somewhere interesting. When you are out, do not be in a hurry. Talk about what your child sees, hears, tastes, touches, and smells. Take time to enjoy all aspects of the journey. Vary your trips to include some of these places:

- Fresh fruit and vegetable stand
- Farm
- Bakery/doughnut shop
- Fire/police station
- Park/playground
- Zoo/circus
- Aquarium/pet store
- Museum
- Public library
- Movie theater
- Bookstore

Encore

Use your outings as ways to introduce new words. Name the things you see that your child may not have vocabulary for yet. When you get home, review what you saw. The next day, reminisce about the trip. See how many details your child remembers.

        © Instructional Fair • TS Denison

The Nose Knows

Nose, nose, jolly red nose;
And what gave you that jolly red nose? . . .
—Traditional Rhyme

Overture

Stimulating all the senses is important in enriching a three-year-old's learning. Distinguishing aromas is a difficult task for children this age but it can be a fun activity.

Performance

Play: To teach your three-year-old how to distinguish between two familiar odors, play "The Nose Knows."
What you will need: A variety of aromatic foods such as banana, orange, vanilla, maple syrup, chocolate chips, coffee, peanut butter, strawberry jam, grape juice, popped corn
How to play: Place two aromatic foods on the table in front of your child. Have him smell both foods. Have him close his eyes. Put one of the foods near his nostrils so he can smell it. Then place it back on the table. When your child opens his eyes, he is to point to the food he thinks he was smelling.

Finale

A more sophisticated version of this game is to have your child close his eyes while you take an unknown food from the refrigerator or cupboard and have him smell it. Trying to identify the food without seeing it first is much more difficult and will take a great deal of practice.

Encore

On other occasions, try playing tasting games. Place two kinds of foods on the table in front of your child. With eyes closed, place a bite-sized piece of one of the foods on your child's tongue. By tasting, he is to guess which of the two foods he ate.

Keeping Track

Milestone	Date	Comments
Can count to three or five		
Can name the primary colors red, yellow, blue		
Understands time concepts: "day" and "night"		
Can follow a series of commands		
Can memorize short nursery rhymes		
Can use a hammer to pound in nails		
Can name body parts: knees, elbows, hips, ankles		
Can sort things by size: small and large		
Can sort things by color: red, blue, or yellow		
Can sort things by shape: circle, triangle, or square		
Can sort by similar attributes: size, shape, and color		
Understands concepts "now" and "later"		
Understands concept of humor and can joke		
Begins to understand "wishes"		
Can learn from new experiences		

© Instructional Fair • TS Denison

PLAYING
With Your Preschooler
Four Years Old

© Instructional Fair • TS Denison

Hands, Fingers, Thumbs

Fine Motor Development

 ### Contemplate

By age four, most children have excellent finger skills and can handle small objects. Their self-care skills include dressing and undressing. They can button and unbutton, lace their shoes, zip up their jackets, fold and put away their own clothes. They can brush their teeth, comb their hair, wash their hands, and dry off with towels. Four-year-olds can usually completely feed themselves. They have no problem using spoons and forks and can easily drink from cups without spilling.

Their newly acquired small motor skills make it possible to accomplish various craft projects. Most four-year-olds can string small beads, cut on a line, and trace large, basic shapes. When creating, they can begin with an idea. When working with clay, they can decide ahead of time what they want to make and then mold that specific shape or object.

When it comes to games, preschoolers like challenges and enjoy play that involves many little pieces such as cards, board games, puzzles, or building with small construction bricks that snap together.

Fine Motor Milestones: Four Years

◆ Can button and unbutton
◆ Can lace shoes
◆ Can stay inside lines when coloring
◆ Can use a paintbrush
◆ Can trace a triangle and other geometric patterns
◆ Can trace some uppercase letters
◆ Can draw people with bodies and details
◆ Can use a spoon, fork, and knife
◆ Can use kitchen tools such as a peeler, rolling pin, and an eggbeater
◆ Can use a glue stick
◆ Can cut along a solid line with scissors
◆ Can paste things together
◆ Can slice things with a plastic serrated knife
◆ Can make a sandwich

© Instructional Fair • TS Denison

General Tips

Most four-year-olds love to help in the kitchen. They especially enjoy preparing food for the family. No matter how tedious the kitchen job may seem, a four-year-old will enjoy completing it. A child this age will spend twenty minutes scrubbing a tabletop or washing dishes and never get bored. When the job is finished, the young child may stand back and admire her work, and enjoy being praised for a job well done.

As a general rule, four-year-olds are extremely interested in crafts, too. They are as excited about the process as the product. They can plan ahead and begin a project with an idea in mind. They take great pride in their accomplishments and enjoy making things to give to others.

Appropriate toys for developing a four-year-old's fine-motor skills include:
◆ Watercolors and brushes
◆ Crayons and coloring books
◆ Paper and pencils with erasers
◆ Puzzles with six or more pieces
◆ Small beads to string
◆ Sewing cards and laces
◆ Card games such as "Old Maid" or "Go Fish"
◆ Dominoes
◆ Small, blunt scissors
◆ Glue sticks
◆ Craft sticks, pipe cleaners, stickers, glitter
◆ Play clay
◆ Plastic, interlocking construction blocks; construction toys
◆ Stamp pads and stamps

Fine Motor Development **Four-Year-Old**

Dressing Relay

Hector Protector was dressed all in green.
Hector Protector was sent to the Queen.
The Queen did not like him, nor did the King.
So Hector Protector was sent back again.
—Traditional Rhyme

Overture

Four-year-olds differ in abilities, but generally speaking most preschoolers can care for themselves by dressing, eating, and grooming themselves.

Performance

Play: To encourage your four-year-old to practice buttoning and unbuttoning, play "Dressing Relay."

What you will need: Two piles of clothes (each including a blouse or shirt with large buttons), boots, hat, gloves or mittens

How to play: The object of the game is to race to see who can put on all of the clothes in his stack first. Clothes should be large enough to fit over regular clothes. Boots should slide on with ease. Buttons must be big enough that the child can button them without assistance. Say, "Ready? Set. Go!" Both race over to a pile of clothes and begin to dress. After you are both dressed, use a full-length mirror to look at yourselves. Then race to see who can undress first.

Finale

To reinforce a skill like lacing a shoe or zipping a jacket, play "Dressing Relay" and include shoes to lace or a jacket to zip. Make sure your child has the opportunity to finish the race first at least half of the time. Four-year-olds love to boast and think of themselves as winners. So each time he wins the race, applaud and cheer him on. Praise him every time he does something well.

Encore

Racing is a good way to get your four-year-old moving. No matter what the task, if there is a race involved, most four-year-olds will cooperate.

- ◆ If he does not want to take a bath, see if he can undress before the water gets to a certain level in the tub.
- ◆ If he does not want to get dressed, see if he can get dressed before the three-minute timer goes off.
- ◆ If he does not want to pick up his toys, put on a tape or CD and see if he can clean up his room before the end of a certain song.
- ◆ If he does not want to get into bed, see if he can get under the covers before you count to six.
- ◆ If he does not want to brush his teeth, see who can get his teeth the cleanest.
- ◆ If he does not want to come into the house, say, "The last one in the house is a rotten egg" and race him to the door.

© Instructional Fair • TS Denison

Lace the Boot

One, two, lace the boot.
Three, four, tie it, too.
Five, six, lickity-split.
Seven, eight, you are great!

Overture

Watch your four-year-old learning and accomplishing new things, and you will see a joyous, exuberant, energetic child. Four-year-olds need to learn to trust their hands, and mastering fine-motor skills is proof to your child that she has things under control.

Performance

Play: To give your four-year-old an opportunity to lace shoes, play "Lace the Boot."
What you will need: A large man's boot with long laces
How to play: Lace the boot up leaving only the two top holes unlaced. Ask your child to finish lacing up the boot. Then unlace two holes on each side and repeat having her lace up the boot. Unlace and lace until your child can complete the task by herself.

Finale

Create personalized sewing cards for lacing practice, too. Cut favorite colorful pictures from magazines. Glue the pictures to sheets of heavy paper or lightweight cardboard. Use a hole punch to make some holes around the edges of the pictures. Use long, colorful shoelaces to connect the holes on the sewing cards.

Encore

Stringing wooden beads (they can be much smaller beads than used previously) is good eye-hand coordination practice for your four-year-old. Giving verbal instructions about the pattern of colors to use when stringing enhances the learning experience. For example, ask your child to string a pattern alternating red, blue, and yellow. Then have your child name the colors of the beads as she strings them.

Inside the Lines

Here we go up, up, up,
Here we go down, down, down,
And here we go backwards and forwards,
And here we go round, round, round.
—Traditional Rhyme

Overture ....

Some parents do not want their children to use coloring books because they feel it will limit the child's creativity. However, used sparingly, coloring books can be good practice staying inside areas, outlining large shapes, and cutting out large bold pictures.

Performance ....

Play: To encourage your child to stay inside the lines when coloring, provide age-appropriate coloring books.
What you will need: Pictures with large areas
How to play: Having your child color inside the lines of a picture is good practice. However, if he does not like to be confined in this way, encourage him to color the picture any way he chooses.

Finale ....

Many four-year-olds enjoy tracing the lines in coloring books. Using a crayon to outline a picture is good eye-hand coordination practice. Choose simple pictures for your child to outline.

Encore ....

While your child is slowly moving a crayon, it is a good time to reinforce directional terms: "up," "down," "around," "forward," "backward," etc. Challenge him on a sheet of paper to draw:

- ◆ A red line "down"
- ◆ A blue line "up"
- ◆ A yellow circle "round and round"
- ◆ A green line "forward"
- ◆ A purple line "backward"
- ◆ An orange line "up and down," and "up and down"

        © Instructional Fair • TS Denison

Paint the "Town" Red

Paint the town red, paint the grass green.
Paint the barn blue and the sky, too.

Overture

Some four-year-olds especially enjoy working with letters and numbers. Children this age do not have to learn to recognize the letters or read words, but working with letters and basic words in an informal way is an excellent introduction to letter recognition skills.

Performance

Play: To give your child practice using a paint-brush to paint, play "Paint the 'Town' Red."

What you will need: Watercolors, paintbrush, large sheet of paper, pencil

How to play: Write a word with 4" (10 cm) tall letters such as "town" on a sheet of paper. Instruct your child to use a specific color to paint the lines and curves in the word. Use a separate sheet for each word.

Examples:

◆ Paint **BARN** blue.

◆ Paint **GRASS** green.

◆ Paint **SKY** blue.

Finale

Another fun activity for painting words is to paint the color words the appropriate color. Example: Paint the word RED with red paint. Paint the word BLUE with blue paint, etc.

Challenge your child to paint the letters of her first name in her favorite colors. (Be sure to print her name using an initial uppercase letter and then lowercase letters. It is important for her to see her name written correctly.) Glue glitter to the letters. Cut out and put the colorful name tag where the whole family can see it.

Encore

Use coloring book pictures with a variety of mediums:

◆ Use watercolors to outline the solid lines of pictures.

◆ Use finger paints to fill in large areas with color.

◆ Use fine-tip markers to outline and broad-tipped markers to fill in large areas with color.

◆ Use colored pencils to outline and color pictures.

◆ Glue paper squares in big sections to make collages.

◆ Use colored chalk (also try wet chalk by dipping and soaking it in water before applying) to color large areas.

Sandpaper Shapes

Dickery, dickery, dare.
The pig flew up in the air;
The man in brown
Soon brought him down,
Dickery, dickery, dare.
—Traditional Rhyme

Overture

Four-year-olds can see shapes in all the things around them. Talk about the basic shapes of everyday things: toothpaste tube, glue bottle, detergent box, doughnuts, books, clouds, leaves, houses, cars, etc. Limit the shapes you discuss to basic shapes: circles, squares, rectangle, and triangles.

Performance

Play: To encourage your four-year-old to trace geometric patterns, play with basic geometric shapes cut out from paper and covered with sand.

What you will need: Large triangle, circle, square, and rectangle cut from heavy paper or light cardboard, white glue, sand

How to play: Smooth white glue on the surface of each cutout. Sprinkle with sand. Let dry. When the glue is dry, shake off the excess sand. Have your child use an index finger to trace the edge of each shape as you name it. Then ask your child to name the shape as he traces the edges.

Finale

When your child knows the names of the four shapes, play a game of guessing the shape without seeing it. Blindfold or have your child close his eyes. Hand him one of the shapes. He is to hold the shape, trace the edges, and then guess which shape he is holding. A more advanced game is to hand him an everyday item, and have him name the object and its basic shape. Example: toothpaste box, orange, book, etc. Besides tracing sandpaper shapes, have your child trace the edges of basic geometric shapes in other ways including:

◆ Paint them with watercolors and a brush.
◆ Outline them with markers.
◆ Glue glitter to the edges of paper shapes.
◆ Trace cardboard patterns on construction paper.
◆ Make sewing cards by punching holes around the edges of shapes with a hole punch, then "sew" around the edges with a shoelace.
◆ Use scissors to fringe the edges of paper shapes.

Encore

Books about shapes offer children an opportunity to learn. Little Simon publishes four books by Jan Pienkowski—*Shapes, ABC, 123,* and *Zoo.* The colorful, primary-style illustrations are especially pleasing to youngsters and with one word on each page, these books will be ones he will soon learn to read.

© Instructional Fair • TS Denison

Sandpaper Alphabet Cards

A, B, C, tumble down D,
The cat's in the cupboard, and can't see me.
—Traditional Rhyme

Overture

Watch, and you will see your four-year-old developing both the muscular control and the concentration she needs to master many precise finger and hand movements.

Performance

Play: To help your child trace some letters of the alphabet, make sandpaper alphabet cards.
What you will need: 5" x 8" (13 x 20 cm) index cards, white glue, sand
How to play: Choose two or three letters of the alphabet, and print the capital and lowercase letter of each on an index card. Then put a stream of glue along the lines. Sprinkle with sand. Set aside to dry. When the glue is dry, shake off the excess sand. Have your child trace the sand letters with her index finger. Ask her to name each letter as she is tracing its outline. Do not try to introduce more than a few letters at a time. After your child has mastered those three letters, choose three new ones and begin the process again. Keep the old cards for review.

Finale

Create a set of 26 alphabet cards. Make a new card each week. Write an uppercase and lowercase letter on each index card. Make each letter card unique and different by gluing things along the outline of the letters that begin with that letter. Some things need to be chopped, diced, sliced, cubed, or crushed before gluing/taping them to the cards. Most cards need to be thrown away after playing with them for a week.
Examples:
- Aa—Almonds or acorns
- Bb—Blue beads, buttons, or beans
- Cc—Cotton or candies
- Dd—Dates or daisy petals
- Ee—Eggshells or eggplant
- Ff—French fries or feathers
- Gg—Green glitter or grain
- Hh—Hearts (paper cutouts)
- Ii—Ice cubes, icing
- Jj—Jacks or jigsaw puzzle pieces
- Kk—Kiwi peels or candy kisses
- Ll—Lemon and lime peels
- Mm—Mints or mud
- Nn—Nickels or nuts
- Oo—Onions, oranges, or oatmeal
- Pp—Pennies or popcorn
- Qq—Quarters
- Rr—Raisins, rice, or red ribbon
- Ss—Spaghetti pasta
- Tt—Tea, toothpicks, or toast
- Uu—"Unhappy" faces
- Vv—Vanilla beans or vegetables
- Ww—Waffles
- Xx—"X"s clipped from magazines
- Yy—Yellow yarn
- Zz—Zebra or zoo pictures, old zippers

Encore

Make alphabet sewing cards using large pieces of tagboard or large index cards. Draw one letter on each card. Use a hole punch to put six to eight holes along the letter's outline. Use a shoelace to sew the shape of the letter. Have your child trace along the shoelace with her index finger as she names the letter. Make one new card each day or every other day.

Drawing the Family

There was a little man and he wooed a little maid,
And he said, "Little maid, will you wed—wed—wed.
I have little more to say than will you, yea or nay? . . ."
—Traditional Rhyme

Overture

Watch as your four-year-old draws a picture of a person. His person may still have a potato-shaped body and not too many details, but it will probably have arms and legs and will be recognizable as a person. As time goes by, your child will add more and more details to his pictures of people.

Performance

Play: To encourage your child to draw pictures of people, have him draw the family.
What you will need: Pencil and paper
How to play: Have your child draw a picture of the people in your family. Talk about the number of people included in the picture. Count the number of people in your family. Have your child tell you about the drawing. Praise his work, and display the drawing where it can be enjoyed by everyone in the family.

Finale

Use mediums besides pencils to draw pictures of people. Provide fine-tip markers, finger paints, watercolors, colored chalk, colored pencils, and crayons. Also encourage your child to use clay to mold each family member.

Encore

Use thumbprints made with an ink pad for the bodies of people. Show your child how to add heads, arms, legs, etc. Also use thumbprints to make animals, flowers, and other objects that have a round center.

Snowperson

One, two, three balls of snow.
Roll 'em, pound 'em,
Pack 'em, stack 'em.
One tall snowman.

Overture

For the average four-year-old, crafts provide an opportunity for her to tell a story. Children this age enjoy creating imaginary worlds with their art and then telling people about what they have created.

Performance

Play: To give your child practice pasting things together, make a paper snowperson picture.

What you will need: Blue and white construction paper, glue stick, hole punch

How to play: Cut or tear three graduating in size circles from the white paper. Encourage your child to glue them to the blue paper so that the largest one is on the bottom and smallest is on top. Use the hole punch to make white dots. Glue them to the picture to represent snowflakes. Picking up and gluing the tiny "snowflakes" will take great eye-hand coordination. A wet paper towel will help keep your child's sticky hands clean while working.

Finale

Pasting various sizes of shapes in order from smallest to largest is good practice. Cut squares, ovals, circles, and triangles in various sizes. Have your child glue them on a sheet of paper in order according to size or in interesting patterns to create collages.

Encore

Creating paper chains by interlacing and gluing ends of paper strips together is fun for most four-year-olds. Strips about 1" (25 mm) wide and 6" (152 cm) long are a good size for small hands. Show your child how to glue the ends of one strip together. Then lace another strip through the loop before gluing its ends together. Continue until your child has made a long chain to hang in her room.

Scissor Hands

Snip, snip, clip, clip.

Overture

When choosing craft materials for a four-year-old, try different kinds, sizes, and colors of paper, and different types of markers, crayons, and chalk. Include blackboards, laminated drawing boards, and a magic slate. Try watercolors and tempera paint. Keep the craft materials all together in a place where your child can work independently.

Performance

Play: To help your child learn how to cut along a solid line, buy coloring books with simple, bold shapes.

What you will need: Coloring books with simple outlined pictures, blunt scissors, construction paper, glue stick, crayons

How to play: Let your child choose a page in a coloring book. Tear it out. Because each child's interests are somewhat different, it is a good idea to let your child help you choose the coloring books. For example, if he likes trains or trucks, look for books that feature a lot of motor vehicles. Make sure the pictures are very simple and easy to cut out. Show your child how to cut around the bold outline of the picture. Glue the picture to a sheet of construction paper. When the glue is dry, color the picture. As simple as this task may sound, your four-year-old may find it very challenging and fun.

Finale

If your child seems to have difficulty using scissors, teach him these steps to follow:
- Hold the scissors at right angles to the paper.
- Use the open and closing motion.
- Control the direction of the scissors by placing the paper so the blades will cut at the appropriate angle.

Basic shapes cut from cardboard can be traced on paper and then cut out. Shapes such as a circle, oval, rectangle, triangle, and square are the best. Stars or complicated shapes may be too difficult for most four-year-olds to cut out. Cookie cutters can also be used for tracing activities. Mugs and small plates will provide good forms for tracing circles.

Encore

For odd shapes to cut out, try leaf rubbings. Leaf rubbings can be done by most four-year-olds. Gather green leaves that will not crumble. Place a sheet of white paper on top of the leaf. Show your child how to use the side of a crayon to rub over the paper. Then cut out the colorful paper leaf. Do a variety of leaf shapes and hang them about the house or in the child's room.

        © Instructional Fair • TS Denison

Dress-Up Lunch

Cross Patch, draw the latch,
Sit by the fire and spin.
Take a cup, and drink it up,
And call your neighbors in.
            —Traditional Rhyme

Overture

Watch, and you will notice that your child not only can feed herself nicely, but she can set the table as well. Children this age should be taking meals with the family and may enjoy the social hour with family members. However, mealtimes longer than 20 minutes may prove difficult for preschoolers.

Performance

Play: To help your child practice using a spoon, knife, and fork to eat, have a dress-up lunch.

What you will need: Set a child-sized table with a cloth cover, china dishes, candles, napkins, spoons, forks, and knives.

How to play: You can teach your child good table manners by including the following:
- ◆ Serve a lunch that needs to be eaten with eating utensils.
- ◆ Show your child how to hold a fork and knife when cutting meat.
- ◆ Show her how to pass food to another person.
- ◆ Show her how to use her napkin and keep it in her lap.
- ◆ Show her how to rest her knife across the top of her plate.

Finale

Setting the table is good practice. Four-year-olds can fold napkins and put plates and eating utensils on the table. When your child is setting the table, use nonbreakable dishes. Have her place one plate on the table at a time. After dinner, she might be able to clear the table or help you load the dishes into the dishwasher. Children this age also like to unload dishwashers and stack the contents on countertops. Children can also sort flatware and put it in drawers.

Encore

Taking your child to restaurants is good practice, too. Begin by taking her to fast-food restaurants for lunch. Use eating utensils even if they are plastic. Show her how to cut a sandwich in half so it is easier to handle. After your child can manage eating in fast-food restaurants, try taking her to a more formal place for lunch and then dinner. Do not expect your four-year-old to be quiet at the table for longer than 20 minutes. If the meal drags on too long and she gets bored, misbehavior may begin.

Bake an Apple Pie

An apple pie, when it looks nice,
Would make one long to have a slice,
But if the taste should prove so, too,
I fear one slice would scarcely do.
So to prevent my asking twice,
Pray, Mamma, cut a good large slice.
—Traditional Rhyme

Overture

Four-year-olds like to do just about anything in the kitchen. Since there are dangerous appliances in the kitchen, it is a place your child can only work when supervised. However, your kitchen may prove to be a very excellent classroom if used with care.

Performance

Play: To teach your child how to use kitchen tools, bake an apple pie together.

What you will need: Pie pan, vegetable peeler, 12 apples, lemon juice, sugar, flour, ready-made pie crust, knife, plastic serrated knife, mixing spoon

How to play: First, have your child wash the apples. For one pie you will need about 12 large apples. Here are the steps your child can help complete:

◆ Wash and dry the apples.
◆ Use a peeler to remove most of the peelings from the apples.
◆ On a cutting board, quarter the apples. Give your child a plastic serrated knife, and let him cut away the core and seeds.
◆ Slice the cored apple quarters again and place in a bowl.
◆ Squeeze the juice of a lemon on the apple slices and stir.
◆ Sprinkle the apples with ¼ cup (59 ml) sugar and ¼ cup (59 ml) flour. Stir.
◆ Put one ready-made crust in the bottom of a pie pan.
◆ Fill the pie crust with the apple mixture.
◆ Place another ready-made crust on top of the apples.
◆ Using fingers and thumb, pinch the edges of the dough together along the edges of the pie pan. Cut a happy face on top.
◆ Bake one hour at 350° F (177° C).

Finale

While the pie is baking, talk about the steps used to make the pie. Play the game "Which Came First?" Ask your child, "Which came first?"

◆ Pinching the edges of the dough or slicing the apples?
◆ Peeling the apples or cutting out the seeds?
◆ Baking the pie or squeezing the lemon juice?
◆ Placing the dough on the apples or washing the apples?

Encore

Encourage your child to make other desserts with apples. Sliced apples sprinkled with sugar and cinnamon, and topped with brown sugar, butter, and instant oatmeal can be cooked in the microwave for one to two minutes to make a great quick apple crisp.

          © Instructional Fair • TS Denison

Instant Pudding

Sing, sing! What shall I sing?
The cat's run away with the pudding-bag string!
—Traditional Rhyme

Overture

Some children, especially older four-year-olds, are interested in cooking. Any task preparing food is motivating for four-year-olds. At meals your child is learning as much about people and relationships as she is about foods. Try to make mealtimes friendly and congenial. When your child creates a special dessert for the family dinner, she will be even more anxious for mealtime.

Performance

Play: To help teach your child how to use kitchen tools such as an eggbeater, make instant pudding.
What you will need: Hand-turned eggbeater, bowl, instant pudding mix, measuring cup, milk
How to play: Have your child help in each step, making the instant pudding.

- ◆ Open the pudding mix.
- ◆ Pour the contents of the pudding mix into a big bowl.
- ◆ Measure the milk according to directions on the package.
- ◆ Add milk to the pudding mix.
- ◆ Use the eggbeater to mix the pudding. Your child can do this. It might take some time, but she will not mind the extra effort.
- ◆ When the pudding begins to get thick, place it in the refrigerator until it sets up.

Finale

Beating whipping cream until it is thick is another good task to give your child practice using a hand-turned eggbeater. Whipping egg whites is more difficult than whipping cream or making pudding, but making meringue is also a task most four-year-olds can accomplish with a little bit of help.

Encore

On other occasions, use a hand-turned eggbeater to make butter icing for cookies or cupcakes.
Butter Icing: Mix 3 tablespoon (45 ml) softened butter, 2½ cups (592 ml) confectioners' sugar, and a drop of water if needed.
Sugar Cookies: Let your child slice a roll of refrigerator dough with a plastic serrated knife. Place each slice on a cookie sheet and bake as directed on the package. When cool, spread on the icing.
Cupcakes: Let your child place the paper baking cups in a muffin pan. Use the hand-turned eggbeater to mix the cake mix as directed on the package. Pour the batter into the paper baking cups. Bake as directed on the package. Cool completely and frost.

Soup's On!

Pease porridge hot,
Pease porridge cold,
Pease porridge in the pot nine days old.
—Traditional Rhyme

Overture

Some tools in the kitchen are dangerous, including knives and can openers. However, if you instruct your child on the proper ways to use these tools and you supervise his tasks, a four-year-old can use these kitchen tools in safe ways. In societies where children are given knives at an early age, they rarely cut themselves. Proper training and supervision is the key to using kitchen tools safely.

Performance

Play: To give your child practice using a hand-turned can opener, let him make soup for lunch.
What you will need: Hand-turned can opener, wooden spoon, can of soup, pan, soup bowls and spoons
How to play: Let your child do most of the steps to make the lunch.
- ◆ Show your child how to close the can opener on the edge (cleaned with soapy water) of the soup can. Repeat several times. Let him try.
- ◆ When the can opener is latched onto the can edge, show him how to turn the handle until the whole lid has been cut off the can.
- ◆ Show him how to reverse the handle to release the lid from the can opener. Carefully remove the lid from the can for your child.
- ◆ Pour the soup into the pan.
- ◆ On low setting, place the pan of soup on the stove. Have your child use the wooden spoon to stir the soup. When the soup is warm and bubbly, pour the soup into the bowls for your child.

Finale

Give your child an opportunity to use the can opener to open other cans, too. Here are some quick lunches your four-year-old can help make:
- ◆ Tuna Salad—Open a can of tuna. Place tuna, mayonnaise, pickle relish, and chopped celery in a bowl and stir. Serve on toast.
- ◆ Chicken Cashew Salad—Open a can of chicken. Place the chicken in a bowl. Add chopped cashews, celery, apples, mayonnaise, and raisins. Serve on a bed of lettuce.
- ◆ Burritos—Open a can of refried beans. Spread on a flour tortilla and sprinkle grated cheese over the top. Fold it over and heat in a microwave.
- ◆ Cherry Cobbler—Open a can of cherry pie filling. Pour it on prepared biscuit mix and sprinkle it with sugar. Bake until the cobbler is set.

Encore

Baking bread and letting your child knead the dough is good fine-motor practice. Thaw a frozen bread loaf, and let your child knead the whole thing on a floured board. Place the kneaded dough in a greased pan. Cover and let it rise for two hours. Knead again, and then place the dough in the greased pan and let it rise again. Bake as directed on the package. When cool, let your child help slice the bread.

© Instructional Fair • TS Denison

Appetizers

"D" was fat Dick,
Who did nothing but eat.
He would leave book and play
For a nice bit of meat.

Overture

Four-year-olds appreciate foods for their different appearances, flavors, and textures. Watch your child choosing different foods. Colorful, especially orange, yellow, red, and green, foods are particularly enjoyable and appreciated by preschoolers.

Performance

Play: To give your preschooler practice slicing things with a knife, begin by making appetizers.
What you will need: Plastic serrated knife, cutting board, luncheon meats and sliced cheese, round toothpicks
How to play: Show your child how to cut the luncheon meat and cheese slices into strips. Layer the meat and cheese strips together and form a loop. Gently poke the toothpick through both layers. Put a cheese and meat strip loop on each toothpick.

Finale

The confidence you give your child by trusting her to use grown-up tools far outweighs the danger of using the tools. Providing learning instructions and supervision is the key to letting four-year-olds use sharp tools. Creating fruit appetizers is another activity that your four-year-old can perform. Provide ripe fruit including any of these:

- ◆ Bananas
- ◆ Ripe pears
- ◆ Seedless grapes
- ◆ Tangerines or other citrus fruits
- ◆ Apples
- ◆ Berries

Have your child wash, peel, and slice the fruit. Grapes and berries can be cut in half. Bananas can be sliced in bite-sized chunks. Citrus can be peeled and torn into sections. Apples are to be sliced and cored. Assemble two or three different kinds of fruit on each toothpick.

Encore

Letting your four-year-old help prepare family meals will give her great satisfaction and a feeling of belonging. Things she can cut up with plastic serrated knives include:

- ◆ Lettuce for salads
- ◆ Celery or carrot sticks
- ◆ Green onion tops and cucumbers for salads
- ◆ Chunks of soft cheese

Sandwiches

Ham and cheese on rye,
Peanut butter and jelly.
Tuna salad on toast.
And a Poor Boy deli.

Overture

One of the best ways to keep your child healthy is to encourage a balanced diet. Watch your child's eating patterns, and you will see that when your child is given a variety of foods during mealtimes, over a period of time, your child will choose a balanced diet.

Performance

Play: To give your child practice creating foods in the kitchen, make sandwiches together.

What you will need: To make peanut butter sandwiches, you will need bread, peanut butter, and any of the following: orange slices, apple slices, chopped celery, raisins, honey, banana, lettuce leaves, mayonnaise, coconut flakes, chopped cashews, dill pickles, sesame seeds, cream cheese, jelly, or sunflower seeds.

How to play: On a cutting board, show your child how to spread the peanut butter on the bread. Discuss some of the imaginative condiments listed above to add to the sandwich. Encourage your child to experiment and taste a different kind of peanut butter sandwich each time.

Finale

Provide a variety of foods for your child to experience. Heighten his delight with foods by letting him help prepare some of his own lunches Another peanut butter sandwich that children like to make is a Peanut Butter Pinwheel Roll-Up. Begin by having your child slice off the crust of three slices of white sandwich bread. On a cutting board, roll the bread flat with a rolling pin. Very carefully spread with peanut butter and jelly. Then roll up and slice two or three times. Place the slices on a plate so the pinwheel of peanut butter and jelly is showing.

Encore

Yet another peanut butter sandwich that kids like to make is a Peanut Butter Checkerboard Sandwich. Cut off the edges of two wheat and two white slices of sandwich-type bread. Spread the bread with peanut butter and jelly. Layer the bread like this: dark, light, dark, light. Cut into three slices. Then flip the middle strip over so there is a row of light, dark, light, and dark slices. Then cut the bread into two strips the other way. Show your child how to flip over every other square of sandwich so there is a checkerboard pattern.

        © Instructional Fair • TS Denison

Keeping Track

Milestone	Date	Comments
Can button and unbutton clothing		
Can lace a shoe		
Can stay inside lines when coloring		
Can trace geometric patterns		
Can trace some uppercase letters		
Can draw people with details		
Can paste things together		
Can cut along a solid line		
Can use a spoon, knife, and fork to eat		
Can use kitchen tools: peelers, knives, rolling pin		
Can use a kitchen tool: hand-held eggbeater		
Can use kitchen tools: knives and can openers		
Can slice cheese and meat with a plastic serrated knife		
Can make a peanut butter sandwich		

All By Myself

Gross Motor Development

 ### Contemplate

Most four-year-olds like to think of themselves as being strong. By this age they have acquired strength and ease in walking and running. Their movements are coordinated and often even graceful. They walk with long, smooth strides and can run, jump, hop, skip, and dance. Many children this age learn to roller skate, and some ride small bicycles if they are equipped with training wheels. Specific motor abilities, both balancing and moving, have improved impressively. Most four-year-olds cannot only walk upstairs using one foot to a step but they can also walk down the steps the same, self-assured way.

Four-year-olds are sometimes described as "out-of-bounds." Most children this age like to hit, kick, throw, run up and down stairs, and career madly about. They slam doors and knock over things. They need to be alerted by adults when things are getting out of hand and steered in a new direction. Lots of outdoor activities will give your child the exercise he needs and provide an opportunity to spend some of his exuberant energy. Use the games in this chapter to celebrate your four-year-old's gross-motor skills.

 ### Gross Motor Milestones: Four Years

◆ Can catch a bounced ball
◆ Can stand and hop on one foot
◆ Can jump down from small heights and land flat-footed
◆ Can catch a ball with both hands
◆ Can hit a ball with a racket
◆ Can judge direction and distance when throwing
◆ Can skip
◆ Can gallop
◆ Can jump rope "blue-bell fashion"
◆ Can dance and keep time to music
◆ Will use hand rails and safely climb steps to play on slides
◆ Can pump himself on a swing
◆ Can use a teeter-totter or seesaw if supervised
◆ Can climb around on jungle gyms

General Tips

Parents play a vital role in developing a child's motor skills. Many skills need to be practiced on equipment. Providing playtime at playgrounds or parks with big equipment is very important for your four-year-old. Remember, preschoolers are daring. They will try to climb too high or jump from unsafe heights, so when they play on equipment they must be constantly supervised. Your child may seem old enough for more responsibility, but when it comes to physical activities, although she has the physical skills, she does not understand the consequences of her actions. Playing games with her will ensure her safety without appearing that you do not trust her. Concentrate on finding physical activities that you and your four-year-old can share.

Preschoolers are not prepared for the involvement of organized sports, but games where they interact, take turns, and share will have long-lasting social benefits. Use sport balls such as youth-size basketballs, foam-like footballs, and soccer balls to throw, catch, and kick. Although the balls are useful for children this age, the game rules for the organized sports are too complicated and may prove frustrating for your four-year-old.

Appropriate toys for developing a four-year-old's gross-motor skills include:
- ◆ Jump rope
- ◆ Small bicycle with training wheels
- ◆ Wagon
- ◆ Roller skates
- ◆ Basketball, football, soccer ball
- ◆ Badminton racket, birdie
- ◆ Beanbags
- ◆ Tennis balls, tennis racket
- ◆ Table tennis paddles and balls
- ◆ Playground equipment
- ◆ Small trampoline
- ◆ Kites
- ◆ Velcro dart game

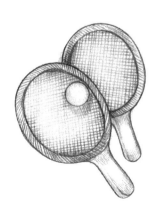

Drop Ball

Dogs in the garden, catch 'em, Towser.
Cows in the cornfield, run, boys, run.
Cats in the cream pot, run, girls, run.
Fire on the mountains, run, boys, run.
—Traditional Rhyme

Overture

Watch to see if sometimes your four-year-old gets so excited about a game that she has difficulty coordinating her hands with her feet. Playing a game several times will give her the practice she needs to coordinate her hands and feet.

Performance

Play: To help your preschooler learn how to catch a bounced ball, play "Drop Ball."
What you will need: Large, soft rubber ball or beach ball
How to play: Standing in front of your child and facing each other, drop the ball. Demonstrate how to use both hands to catch the ball as it bounces upward. This is a difficult skill and may take some time for your child to learn. If this is awkward for your child, signal her at the appropriate time by saying "Catch." Another way to teach her to catch the ball is to put both her arms under the ball as it bounces up and bring it into her chest. Practice catching a bouncing ball. Emphasize the joy of the game, not the catching of the ball.

Finale

Use the rhyme to practice catching a bounced ball. You drop the ball and your child catches it and runs away.

Dogs in the garden, (*Drop the ball.*)
catch 'em, Towser. (*Catches the ball.*)
Cows in the cornfield, (*Drop the ball.*)
run, boys, run. (*Catches the ball and runs around you.*)
Cats in the cream-pot, (*Drop the ball.*)
run, girls, run. (*Catches the ball and runs around you.*)
Fire on the mountains, (*Drop the ball.*)
run, boys, run. (*Catches the ball and runs around you.*)

Encore

On other occasions, encourage your child to bounce and catch the ball by herself. Show her how to bounce a ball off the wall of a building and catch it.

         © Instructional Fair • TS Denison

Hopscotch

Hop away, skip away,
My baby wants to play.
—Traditional Rhyme

Overture

Watch your four-year-old playing boisterous, rough-and-tumble games. Most four-year-olds like this kind of play a lot. Playing games with very simple rules such as "Hopscotch" is a good way to help your child socialize and eventually learn to play games that call for more complicated game rules.

Performance

Play: Give your preschooler an opportunity to practice standing on one foot and hopping by playing "Hopscotch."

What you will need: Smooth stone for each player and the hopscotch pattern drawn on a sidewalk with chalk or taped on a floor with masking tape.

How to play: Standing at the front of the Hopscotch, bend down and toss the stone into the square marked with numeral "1." Then hop into the square marked with numeral "2." Single blocks need a hop and double blocks are a flat-footed resting place. Feet are not to touch the lines. When a player reaches the last space, she is to hop around and hop back again. Remember to not hop into the square with a stone.

Finale

Use the hopscotch area to play other games. Instead of hopping into each square on one foot try:

- ◆ Hopping with two feet together in order 1 to 10 and back again.
- ◆ Walking backward
- ◆ Hopping on tiptoes

Encore

Use the hopscotch area as a beanbag target. Provide beanbags in two different colors. To score points, the bags may not touch a line. Take turns tossing the beanbags. As the beanbag lands, name the numeral shown in that square. To see who wins, count the beanbags which land inside the squares.

Jumping Jack

Jack be nimble, Jack be quick.
Jump, Jack, Jump!

Overture..

Watch your four-year-old at play. Is he often reckless and does he try to jump from high places? Practice jumping with your child so that he will learn how to land without hurting himself.

Performance..

Play: To help your child safely jump down from small heights and land flat-footed, begin by practicing jumping from safe heights.
What you will need: Platform that is 6–10 inches (15–25 cm) off the ground
How to play: Show your child how to stand flat-footed on the edge of the platform. The first few times, hold both his hands while he jumps. After practicing, he will be able to jump without holding your hands. Use the rhyme to signal when he is to jump.

Jack be nimble, Jack be quick.
Jump, Jack, Jump!

Finale ....

Personalize the rhyme, and use it to signal your child to jump over lines drawn 4–6 inches (10–15 cm) apart on the sidewalk.

(Child's name) be nimble,
(Child's name) be quick.
Jump, (child's name), Jump!

Encore ....

Set up an obstacle course. Draw a 12 inch (31 cm) winding course with chalk on a sidewalk. Draw basic shapes inside the course. As your child moves along the course, give him commands such as:
◆ Jump over the square.
◆ Jump into the circle.
◆ Hop inside the triangle.
◆ Stop on the star.
On another occasion, let your child help you invent a different kind of course. Use chalk-drawn symbols on the course to represent different ways to move.
◆ March in place.
◆ Spin around.
◆ Hop on one foot.
◆ Stomp really hard.
◆ Tiptoe softly.

        © Instructional Fair • TS Denison

Catch with a Mitt

. . . when pleasure can be had,
it is fit to catch it.
—Samuel Johnson

Overture

Before age four, most children have difficulty catching small balls. Watch, and you will see that now your child has the eye-hand coordination to catch even small balls. A good way to begin catching balls is to use a baseball mitt, and the more practice she gets catching, the easier it will be for her.

Performance

Play: To give your four-year-old an opportunity to catch a ball, play "Catch" with a tennis ball.
What you will need: Baseball mitt, tennis balls
How to play: Stand about 6 feet (1.8 m) from your child. Give her a small baseball mitt to wear. Gently toss the tennis ball into the baseball mitt. Then have her toss it back to you. Practice at this distance. Then back up to 8 feet (2.4 m) and eventually to 10 feet (3 m). Catching and tossing balls is excellent eye-hand coordination as well as gross-motor practice.

Finale

Beanbag catch is also good practice for four-year-olds. If your child is afraid of a ball, practice catching with beanbags filled with pieces of foam packing. It will be light enough that it will not hurt, even if it hits her, and yet heavy enough to toss back and forth. Progress to a slightly heavier beanbag by filling it with rice or small round pasta. Also encourage your child to play alone by tossing a beanbag up and then catching it.

Encore

Tossing and catching is great fun, and it is a game that can be played a multitude of ways. Look around, and you will see all kinds of things that you can use as a ball. Incorporate other catching games into you and your child's daily routine:
   ◆ When folding laundry, toss rolled-up socks back and forth.
   ◆ When picking up toys, toss a stuffed animal back and forth.
   ◆ When getting ready for a bath, toss a damp washcloth back and forth.
   ◆ When cleaning the kitchen, toss a dish towel tied in a knot back and forth.
   ◆ When putting away groceries, stuff a plastic bag with more plastic bags, close it with a knot, and toss it back and forth.
   ◆ When working in the yard, toss a small bag of leaves back and forth.
   ◆ When cleaning the garage, toss a rolled-up newspaper back and forth.
   ◆ When cleaning out a desk, toss a wad of paper back and forth.
   ◆ When washing the car, toss a wet sponge back and forth.

Wall Tennis

Trip and go, heave and ho!
Up and down, to and fro; . . .
—Traditional Rhyme

Overture..

Using sticks, bats, or rackets as extensions of the arms to play with balls takes a great deal of coordination. Watch, and you will see that the more practice your child has with bats and rackets the more quickly he will learn to coordinate them with the ball.

Performance..

Play: To teach your child how to hit a ball with a racket, play "Wall Tennis."
What you will need: Plastic tennis racket, inflated balloon
How to play: Show your child how to gently hit the balloon with the tennis racket against a smooth outside wall. Hit the balloon against the wall, and let your child try to hit it back with his racket. Tap the balloon back and forth against the wall.

Finale...

Try playing volleyball indoors with an inflated balloon. No net is needed. Take turns hitting the balloon up in the air, back and forth. When you cannot be there to volley the balloon to your child, show him how to repeatedly hit it up to see how long he can keep it airborne. Other things that your child can try to volley include:

◆ Paper wad
◆ Beanbag
◆ Large feather
◆ Plastic bag filled with Styrofoam pieces
◆ Plastic grocery bag filled with plastic bags

Encore ....

For coordination practice using extensions to hit balls, try some of these:

◆ Try batting large whiffle balls with a fat plastic bat.
◆ Try batting a small beach ball with a thin plastic bat.
◆ Use the tube from a long roll of gift wrap to "putt" rolled-up socks along the floor or grass.
◆ Use a child-sized broom to "putt" paper wads.

       © Instructional Fair • TS Denison

Bull's-Eye Games

In the long run men hit only what they aim at.
—Henry David Thoreau

Overture

Your child's thought process is expanding. A year ago she ran aimlessly about, now at four years of age she will think ahead and have something in mind before she leaps. Watch, and you will see that she often moves with purpose.

Performance

Play: To give your child practice judging direction and distances when throwing, play "Bull's-Eye Games."

What you will need: Velcro dartboard and Velcro darts

How to play: Hang the Velcro dartboard on the wall about 4 feet (1.2 cm) off the ground. Have your child stand approximately 6 feet (1.8 m) from the target. Take turns throwing the darts.

Finale

Bull's-eye games are good practice for judging direction and distances. "Erase the Face" is a wet sponge bull's-eye game played outside. Create the target by drawing a silly face with chalk on a large chalkboard or side of a cement wall. (The wall can be hosed down afterwards to remove any chalk marks.) Have your child stand about 6 feet (1.8 m) away from the target. Throw wet sponges at the target to erase the face. How long or how many throws does it take for your child to erase the face? A bucket of water will help keep the sponge wet.

Encore

Create a target with a large sheet of cardboard. Draw a clown's face on the cardboard. Use a straight edge to cut out the clown's nose and mouth. Hang the cardboard face from a clothesline. Standing about 6 feet (1.8 m) away from the target, have your child try to toss tennis balls or beanbags through the clown's nose and mouth. When your child gets good at her aim, have her try throwing the balls or beanbags underhand, overhand, or bending over and throwing from between her legs.

Skip to My Lou

Skip, skip, skip to my Lou,
Skip, skip, skip to my Lou,
Skip, skip, skip to my Lou,
Skip to my Lou, my Darling.
—Traditional Song

Overture

Four-year-olds become very smooth in their movements. Watch, as with practice, your child's running, hopping, skipping, and galloping will become effortless.

Performance

Play: To give your child practice skipping, play "Skip to My Lou."
What you will need: No special equipment is needed to play this game.
How to play: If your child is not familiar with the skipping movement, begin by demonstrating and explaining. Skipping is a little hop on one foot and then repeating on the opposite foot while moving forward. Skip in place for practice until the alternating hop is mastered. Then have your child try to move forward while skipping. For some children, it is easier to learn to skip with the hop on the right or the left foot only.

Finale

When your child can skip, use the rhyme to keep a skipping beat.

Skip, (*Skip on right foot*)
skip, (*Skip on left foot*)
skip (*Skip on right foot*)
to my Lou, (*Skip on left foot*)
Skip, (*Skip on right foot*)
skip, (*Skip on left foot*)
skip (*Skip on right foot*)
to my Lou, (*Skip on left foot*)
Skip, (*Skip on right foot*)
skip, (*Skip on left foot*)
skip (*Skip on right foot*)
to my Lou, (*Skip on left foot*)
Skip (*Skip on right foot*)
to my Lou, (*Skip on left foot*)
my (*Skip on right foot*)
Darling. (*Skip on left foot*)

Encore

Skipping is like smiling; it will put your child in a happy mood. Skip to music with your child. Encourage your child to skip by having skipping races and playing skipping tag games.

© Instructional Fair • TS Denison

Wild Pony

This is the way the wild pony runs,
Gallop-a-trot, gallop-a-trot.
This is the way the wild pony runs,
Gallop-a-trot, gallop-a-trot.

Overture

Shared physical activities like skipping and galloping have the qualities of games. Be playful with your child. Knowing how to have fun is one of the most important things you can model for your preschooler.

Performance

Play: To help introduce and reinforce the galloping movement, play "Wild Pony."
What you will need: No special equipment is needed to play this game.
How to play: The term "gallop" comes from the way a horse runs. Gallop means to lead with one leg. Demonstrate a gallop (run leading with right foot). Then gallop leading with the left foot.

Finale

After your child knows how to gallop, pretend to be wild ponies. Pinning a scarf to the back of your collar (for a mane) and the bottom of shirt (for a tail) may make the galloping game more fun. Recite the rhyme, and gallop to a beat. Making the "neighing" sound of a horse will also add to the excitement of being a "wild pony."

Encore

Four-year-olds usually like everything about ponies. Include some of these in your play:
- ◆ Get on all fours, and let him sit on your back as if he is riding a pony.
- ◆ Carry him piggy-back style and gallop around the house with him on your back.
- ◆ Visit a place where your child can ride a real pony.
- ◆ Ride ponies on a merry-go-round.

Blue Bells

Blue bells, cockle shells,
Evy, ivy, over.

Overture..

Jump rope is a difficult skill. Turning the rope and jumping at just the right time takes a great deal of coordination and practice and is not learned by most children until they are five, six, or even seven years old. However, you can teach your child to jump a rope blue-bell fashion.

Performance..

Play: To introduce rope jumping, play "Blue Bells."
What you will need: Long, heavy cotton rope; two people to hold the ends of the rope or a post to tie one end while you hold the other end
How to play: Two rope turners stand 6–8 feet (1.8–2.4 m) apart holding the ends of the rope. Blue Bells is a form of jump rope where the rope is moved back and forth instead of overhead. The child stand in the middle, and as the rope is moved back and forth, she jumps over it. The back and forth movement of the rope should be only an inch (2.5 cm) off the ground. In the beginning, the rope can be held still while the child jumps over it, back and forth from one side of the rope to the next. When your child can jump the rope when moved back and forth very slowly, recite the rhyme as you play.

> Blue bells, (*Jump over the rope.*)
> Cockle shells, (*Jump over the rope the other way.*)
> Evy, (*Jump over the rope.*)
> Ivy, (*Jump over the rope the other way.*)
> Over. (*Turn the rope over the child's head, and she jumps one more time.*)

Finale..

Use other rhymes to jump rope. Use the back-and-forth method instead of over the head. Begin by holding the rope only 1 inch (2.5 cm) off the ground.

> Cinderella, (*Jump over the rope.*)
> Dressed in yellow. (*Jump back over the rope.*)
> Went to town (*Jump over the rope.*)
> To find her fellow. (*Jump back over the rope.*)
> How many miles (*Jump over the rope.*)
> Must she go? (*Jump back over the rope.*)
> One, (*Raise the rope 1 inch [2.5 cm] before the child jumps.*)
> Two, (*Raise the rope another inch [2.5 cm] before the child jumps.*)
> Three, (*Raise the rope another inch [2.5 cm] before the child jumps.*)
> Four . . . (*Count and raise until the child cannot jump over the rope without touching it.*)

Encore...

When you cannot be there to hold the rope, tie a long piece of elastic between two chairs or trees an inch (2.5 cm) off the ground. That way your child can practice jumping alone.

         © Instructional Fair • TS Denison

Move to the Music

Hark! Hark! The dogs do bark, the beggars have come to town,
Some in rags, and some in tags, and some in velvet gowns.
—Traditional Rhyme

Overture

Most four-year-olds love to dance, march, and move to music. Dancing is an excellent way to expose your child to sounds of different cultures while celebrating large motor movement. Watch your child moving to music; what are his favorite sounds?

Performance

Play: To teach your child how to move and keep time to music, exercise with music playing in the background.

What you will need: Slow, flowing music on CD or audiotape; audiotape or CD player

How to play: Play the music. Stretch a variety of body parts as you demonstrate the following exercises:

◆ Flying—Flap arms up and down like a big bird. Touch the palms of hands overhead and then all the way down to the sides of body, move arms up and down, up and down. (This exercise is the upper body part of jumping jacks.)

◆ Salute to the Sun—Bend over at the waist, and touch the floor with the palms of hands, then slowly rise and stand tall. Use the arms to form a circle (the sun) above the head.

◆ Twist in the Wind—Stand tall. Twist the body at the waist all the way around as far as possible to one side, then back to the original position. Then twist the body all the way around in the other direction and back again. Repeat.

◆ Turtle—Stand tall, then bend the head down to the chest. Look to the right. Look to the left. Slowly move the head back and forth as if you are a turtle stretching its neck.

◆ Butterfly—This movement is to represent a butterfly emerging from a cocoon. Bend the head forward, bring the arms over the head with elbows touching. Slowly bring the arms out to the sides and down while lifting the head. Flap the arms and "fly" away.

Finale

To exercise the lower body, try these exercises:

◆ Bicycle—Lie on your back and put your legs up in the air. Pretend to pedal a bike.

◆ Elevator—Lie on your back with your legs in the air. Bend your knees. Raise and lower your legs to the music.

◆ Crab Walk—Lie on your back. Bend your knees, lift your body up off the floor, and balance on your feet and hands. With belly up, crawl like a crab.

◆ Snowball—Lie on your back. Bend at the waist, and use your hands to bring your lower body up off the floor. Bring your toes overhead. Touch the floor with your toes over your head.

◆ Pill Bug Walk—Holding onto your ankles, walk to the other side of the room.

◆ Running in Place—Count to twenty as your child runs in place.

Encore

On other occasions, exercise the legs by marching to music such as John Philip Sousa marches. Use big, high-stepping movements. Move slow. Move fast.

One Step Up

. . . One foot up, the other foot down,
And that is the way to London town.
—Traditional Rhyme

Overture

Watch your child demonstrating her strength. Learning to trust her own hands and feet to keep her from falling will empower your preschooler. Encourage your child to trust her own grasp by having her hold onto the railings while climbing the steps on slides.

Performance

Play: To encourage your four-year-old to hold the railings and safely climb the steps of a slide, play "One Step Up."

What you will need: Slide

How to play: Standing at the bottom of the slide steps, show her how to hold the railings with both hands. Then as she climbs up the steps she is to let go of only one hand at a time. When she gets to the top of the slide, instruct her to hold onto the railings while she is sitting down. Only when she feels balanced and ready to slide down should she let go of the railings with both hands. If she wants a slower ride down the slide, she can again use her hands on the edges of the slide to slow down her momentum.

Finale

Using an escalator is another time when preschoolers should be taught to hold the railing. When visiting a shopping center that has escalators, have your child ride an escalator and practice using the handrails.

Encore

Handrails should be used when your child climbs up or down stairs. Practice walking up and down stairs using the handrails. When you are shopping in a mall or visiting a professional office that is located on a second floor, instead of taking the elevator, practice using the handrails and climb the stairs.

© Instructional Fair • TS Denison

Swing Up High

Swing up high; reach for the sky.
Swing up high; you can fly.

Overture

Whether it is a swing set in the backyard or the more elaborate swings found in parks, there are many positive things your child will experience while swinging. Pumping a swing is a good upper body and full body balancing exercise. Watch to see if your child can pump herself on a swing.

Performance

Play: Teach your child how to pump herself in a swing so she can swing even when there is no one there to push her.

What you will need: Swing made with soft and flexible materials

How to play: Show your preschooler how to sit in the middle of the seat and hold on with both hands. Stand behind her and gently push. When you want to teach your preschooler how to pump a swing so she can propel herself back and forth, demonstrate what to do while she watches. Then put her in the swing, and talk her through the steps.

◆ While swinging backward, tuck the legs up under the body and lean forward slightly.
◆ When moving forward, push the legs out straight in front of the body and lean backward.

Have her try the steps as you verbally guide her. When your child can pump herself in a swing, you are ready to play, "Swing Up High."

Finale

To play "Swing Up High" place your child in a swing, stand behind her, and push to get her swinging. When she is pumping the swing on her own, move around in front of her. Then step back and as she pumps herself, back up so that she can barely touch your extended hands. Challenge her to pump the swing higher and higher by stepping back just out of her reach.

Encore

Other swinging games include:
◆ Swinging Races—Swing along side your child and see who can swing the highest.
◆ Counting—Count as the swing moves forward. Then count as it swings backward.
◆ Swinging Together—Swing beside your child and see if the two of you can keep perfect time by swinging back and forth at the same time.

  121

Teeter-Totter

Hiram Gordon, where's your pa?
He's gone with Uncle Peter,
To put a board across the fence,
So that we boys can teeter.
—Traditional Rhyme

Overture

Although teeter-totters or seesaws are not appropriate for three-year-olds, most four-year-olds have the arm and leg coordination and balance to use smaller ones. However, a teeter-totter is playground equipment that needs to be used with assistance from an adult.

Performance

Play: To help your four-year-old learn how to use a teeter-totter safely, give him instructions, demonstrations, and plenty of supervised time on the equipment.

What you will need: Teeter-totter

How to play: Have your child sit on one end of the teeter-totter. Show him how to hold on tightly with both hands. Sit forward on your end of the teeter-totter so that your weight is balanced. Move up and down very slowly at first. When it is time to end the ride, stand up while straddling the teeter-totter and let the other end gently touch the ground. Hold it steady while your child gets off.

Finale

Using a teeter-totter is a unique way of learning about balance. When using the equipment with your child ask questions:

◆ What would happen if you and a friend both got on your end of the teeter-totter?
◆ What would happen if I slid closer to the end on my end?
◆ What would happen if I sat closer to the middle of the teeter-totter?
◆ Why is it important for both people to know when one person is getting off?

Encore

Make balance scales with blocks and cardboard strips. Have your child use them to experiment and compare weights of different toys.

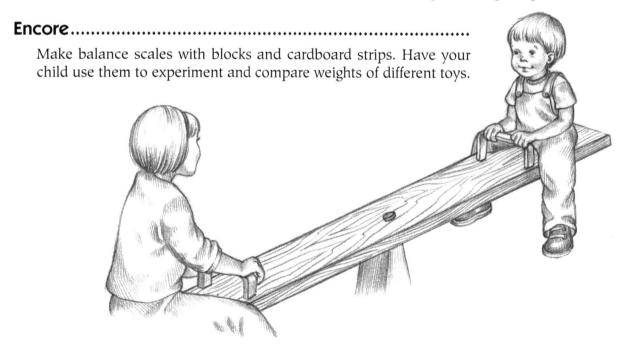

        © Instructional Fair • TS Denison

Jungle Gym Fun

Monkey see,
Monkey do.

Overture

Climbing on jungle gyms relieves stress, builds healthy bodies, and helps improve coordination. Watch your four-year-old climbing on a jungle gym and you will see pure joy in motion.

Performance

Play: To encourage your child to climb around on a jungle gym, play "Jungle Gym Fun."
What you will need: Jungle gym
How to play: Have your child pretend to be an animal like a monkey climbing up and down and all around on the jungle gym. Then instruct him to use movements including:

◆ Climb to the top if the structure is not too tall.
◆ Sit on a bar and shake different body parts as you name them: head, one hand, one foot, etc.
◆ Sit on the ground under the jungle gym and move body parts in different directions as you name them.

Finale

While your child climbs on the jungle gym, give directions including:

◆ Freeze.
◆ Climb up.
◆ Climb down.
◆ Climb across.
◆ Hold on to a bar with both hands and let your body hang free.

Encore

Climbing is good exercise for your four-year-old. Give him the experience of supervised climbing on things besides jungle gyms including:

◆ Hills
◆ Playground wooden forts designed for climbing
◆ Large boulders and rocks

A Movie—Of Me?

See what I can do.
See what I can be.
Are you looking?
Watch me!

Overture

Four-year-olds have an exceptional interest in motor activities. They have better control of their legs and like to try athletic feats. Watch, and you will see that your child's favorite activity will be the one she gets the most attention for doing. Give her lots of praise for her mastery of many gross-motor skills.

Performance

Play: To watch your child's progress as she masters different gross motor skills, create a video of your child's accomplishments.

What you will need: a camcorder and videotape

How to play: Make a video of your child doing some of the motor skill activities she has been learning this year including:

- ◆ Catching a bounced ball
- ◆ Standing on one foot
- ◆ Jumping down from small heights and landing flat-footed
- ◆ Jumping up in the air and landing flat-footed
- ◆ Catching a ball with hands
- ◆ Throwing a ball overhand with a horizontal motion
- ◆ Throwing at and hitting a target
- ◆ Volleying an inflated balloon
- ◆ Hitting a birdie with a badminton racket
- ◆ Climbing steps to play on slides
- ◆ Pumping herself on a swing
- ◆ Using a teeter-totter
- ◆ Climbing on a jungle gym

Finale

Watch the video together. Have your child name the different ways she is moving in the video. Talk about all of the wonderful ways your child can move. On a second viewing, play music and encourage your child to move along with the video. Let her use the movie as her own personal exercise video.

Encore

Let your child know how proud you are of her new motor skills by showing the video to family and friends. Review the video in a year to see how much she is growing and changing.

         © Instructional Fair • TS Denison

Keeping Track

Milestone	Date	Comments
Can catch a bounced ball		
Can safely jump from small heights		
Can catch a small ball with hands		
Can hit a ball with a racket		
Can judge direction and distances when throwing		
Can skip		
Can gallop		
Can jump rope "blue-bell fashion"		
Can dance and keep time to music		
Can use handrails and climb steps of slides		
Can pump him/herself on a swing		
Can use a teeter-totter if supervised		
Can climb on a jungle gym		

Chatter Boxes

Language Development

Contemplate

Just like their fine- and gross-motor skills, four-year-old's language skills will improve with leaps and bounds this year. The more language your child acquires, the more she will be able to think and reason. Children at this age are language oriented.

The two most important things you can do to advance your child's language skills is to talk to her and read to her. Stories based on rhymes such as Dr. Seuss books and stories based on rhythm like nursery rhymes are good for four-year-olds. A list of age-appropriate nursery rhyme books and Dr. Seuss books is found on page 127. Use the games and activities in this chapter to introduce and reinforce language sills.

Language Milestones: Four Years

- ◆ Will follow directions that include adverbs (softly, loudly, quickly, slowly, etc.)
- ◆ Will be able to remember the words and recite rhymes
- ◆ Will be able to sing simple songs
- ◆ Will enjoy learning and reciting tongue twisters
- ◆ Will enjoy participating in the telling of long, repetitive stories
- ◆ Will make up dialogue to perform impromptu plays
- ◆ May speak of imaginary situations
- ◆ Will ask "How?" often and want to hear the explanation
- ◆ Will verbalize similarities and differences
- ◆ Will understand some rules of grammar
- ◆ Will use past, present, and future tenses
- ◆ Will give name and age
- ◆ May be able to give home address
- ◆ Will be able to use language to think in creative ways
- ◆ Will enjoy hearing herself talk

General Tips

To develop language skills, read to your four-year-old, especially age-appropriate nursery rhyme books. The following titles are good selections:

◆ *Animal Crackers: A Delectable Collection of Pictures, Poems, and Lullabies for the Very Young,* designed by Jane Dyer (Little Brown & Co., 1996)

◆ *Ashley Bryan's ABC of African American Poetry: A Jean Karl Book,* edited by Ashley Bryan (Atheneum, 1997)

◆ *Finger Rhymes,* collected and illustrated by Marc Tolon Brown (Puffin, 1996)

◆ *Hand Rhymes,* collected and illustrated by Marc Tolon Brown (Puffin, 1993)

◆ *My Very First Mother Goose,* edited by Iona Archibald Opie (Candlewick Press, 1996)

◆ *The New Adventures of Mother Goose: Gentle Rhymes for Happy Times* by Bruce Lansky (Meadowbrook Press, 1993)

◆ *The Real Mother Goose Board Book,* illustrated by Blanche Fisher Wright (Cartwheel Books, 1998)

◆ *Richard Scarry's Best Mother Goose Ever (Golden Books),* illustrated by Richard Scarry (Golden Press, 1970)

◆ *Skip Across the Ocean: Nursery Rhymes from Around the World,* edited by Floella Benjamin (Orchard Books, 1995)

◆ *Tomie dePaola's Mother Goose,* illustrated by Tomie dePaola (Putnam, 1985)

To enrich your child's speech patterns and build early literacy skills, read books to him based on rhyming words. Dr. Seuss books (Random House) are especially good for presenting interesting rhymes. Dr. Seuss wrote over 50 children's books and illustrated them as well. Dr. Seuss titles include:

◆ *Bartholomew and the Oobleck* (1949)

◆ *The Butter Battle Book* (1984)

◆ *The Cat in a Hat* (1957)

◆ *Daisy-Head Mayzie* (1995)

◆ *The 500 Hats of Bartholomew Cubbins* (1989)

◆ *Hunches in Bunches* (1982)

◆ *I Can Lick 30 Tigers Today, and Other Stories* (1969)

◆ *If I Ran the Circus* (1956)

◆ *If I Ran the Zoo* (1989)

◆ *Kings' Stilts* (1998)

◆ *McElligot's Pool* (1966)

◆ *On Beyond Zebras* (1980)

◆ *One Fish Two Fish Red Fish Blue Fish* (1981)

◆ *Thidwick the Big-Hearted Moose* (1987)

◆ *And to Think I Saw It on Mulberry Street* (Reissue edition, 1989)

Language Development Four-Year-Old

Move It!

Touch your elbows; move your nose.
Bow your head; wiggle your toes.

Overture

Watch your child, and you may be surprised at what a good listener she is becoming. Four-year-olds absorb new words like sponges. They learn language through listening to others.

Performance

Play: To give your four-year-old an opportunity to respond to directions that include adverbs, play "Move It!"

What you will need: No special equipment is needed for this game.

How to play: Have your child listen to your commands and move around the room in a variety of ways. Include these:

- ◆ Walk slowly.
- ◆ Stomp loudly.
- ◆ Skip lightly.
- ◆ Hop quickly.
- ◆ Walk like a sad clown.
- ◆ Run backward.

On another occasion, reverse the game. You move in different ways, and have your child describe the ways you are moving. Encourage her to use adverbs. If she says, you are stomping, ask, "How am I stomping?"

Finale

Four-year-olds are fascinated with mechanical devices. They like to move like machines. Begin by walking around the house and watching the movements made by the washing machine, dryer, toaster, clock, trash compactor, garbage disposal, car window, bicycle, etc. Then name some machines and have your child make the same movements that each machine makes. Finally, have your child try to use words to describe the movements.

Encore

Another game you can play to encourage listening is to have your child stand perfectly still. Play some music. Name one or two body parts and ask her to move only those parts to the beat of the music. Include the following:

- ◆ Hands/feet
- ◆ Arms/elbows
- ◆ Lips/tongue
- ◆ Stomach/back
- ◆ Head/shoulders
- ◆ Legs/knees
- ◆ Eyebrows/eye lids
- ◆ Waist/hips

© Instructional Fair • TS Denison

Teddy Bear

Teddy bear, teddy bear, turn around.
Teddy bear, teddy bear, touch the ground.
Teddy bear, teddy bear, climb the stairs.
Teddy bear, teddy bear, say your prayers.
Teddy bear, teddy bear, turn out the light.
Teddy bear, teddy bear, say "Good night."
—Traditional Rhyme

Overture

Listen to your four-year-old. Does he seem to chatter endlessly? Constant chatter can be tiring for parents. You can, however, redirect his verbal energy by teaching him some limericks or songs.

Performance

Play: To encourage your preschooler to recite rhymes from memory, teach him the words to "Teddy Bear."

What you will need: No special equipment is needed to play this game.

How to play: Begin by saying the rhyme as you and your child perform the appropriate movements together. Then have your child say the rhyme with you as the two of you perform the movements. Finally, have your child recite the rhyme alone while the two of you perform the appropriate movements. Remember, the order of the rhyme can vary.

Teddy bear, teddy bear, turn around. (*Turn around.*)
Teddy bear, teddy bear, touch the ground. (*Stoop and touch the ground.*)
Teddy bear, teddy bear, climb the stairs. (*Pantomime walking up stairs.*)
Teddy bear, teddy bear, say your prayers. (*Kneel.*)
Teddy bear, teddy bear, turn out the light. (*Stand up and pantomime turning off a light switch.*)
Teddy bear, teddy bear, say "Good night." (*Throw a kiss and wave.*)

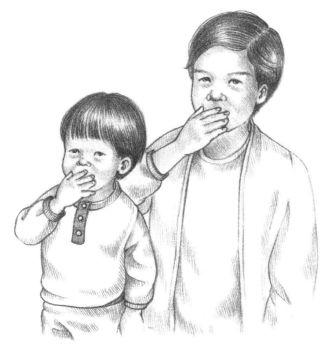

Finale

Another good rhyme to teach your four-year-old and use as an action song is "Little Jack Horner."

Little Jack Horner sat in a corner, (*Sit down and hold a pretend pie.*)
Eating a Christmas pie; (*Pretend to eat pie.*)
He put in his thumb, (*Stick in thumb.*)
And pulled out a plum, (*Pull out the thumb.*)
And said, (*Pause*)
"What a good boy am I!" (*Let your child say the line.*)

Encore

Encourage your child to invent actions for other nursery rhymes that you share with him. After reading a rhyme out loud, have your child pretend to be a character in the rhyme as you recite the rhyme again.

Sing a Song of Sixpence

Sing a song of sixpence,
A pocket full of rye; . . .
—Traditional Rhyme

Overture...

Watch your four-year-old. Does she tend to be bossy and like to be in charge? Giving your child opportunities to lead in play will help meet her need to dominate. When teaching your child an action song, ask her to invent her own actions.

Performance..

Play: To encourage your preschooler to memorize and sing simple songs, teach her the nursery rhyme song, "Sing a Song of Sixpence." Then use it as an action song.

What you will need: No special equipment is needed for this game.

How to play: Sing the song "Sing a Song of Sixpence." Then introduce the actions for each line and recite it again with the actions.

Sing a song of sixpence, (*Clap four times.*)
A pocket full of rye. (*Pat pockets four times.*)
Four-and-twenty blackbirds (*Flap arms four times.*)
Baked in a pie. (*Move arms as if rolling dough.*)
When the pie was opened, (*Open hands and arms wide.*)
The birds began to sing. (*Sing "Tweet, tweet, tweet, tweet."*)
Wasn't that a dainty dish (*Put both hands on hips and tip head.*)
To set before the king? (*Open hands and arms wide again.*)

Finale...

Another nursery rhyme to teach your child to sing is "Mary Had a Little Lamb."
Mary had a little lamb, little lamb, little lamb,
Mary had a little lamb, with fleece as white as snow.
Everywhere that Mary went, Mary went, Mary went,
Everywhere that Mary went, the lamb was sure to go.

It followed her to school one day, school one day, school one day,
It followed her to school one day, which was against the rules.
It made the children laugh and play, laugh and play, laugh and play,
It made the children laugh and play, to see a lamb at school.

And so the teacher turned it out, turned it out, turned it out,
And so the teacher turned it out, but still it lingered near.
The lamb stayed patiently about, patiently about, patiently about,
The lamb stayed patiently about, till Mary did appear.

"Why does the lamb love Mary so, Mary so, Mary so?"
"Why does the lamb love Mary so?" the eager children cried.
"Why, Mary loves the lamb, you know, lamb, you know, lamb, you know,
Mary loves the lamb, you know," the teacher did reply.

Encore..

"Row, Row, Row Your Boat," is another good song to teach your preschooler.

         © Instructional Fair • TS Denison

Twisting Tongues

Peter, Peter, pumpkin-eater,
Had a wife and couldn't keep her.
Put her in a pumpkin shell,
And there he kept her very well.
—Traditional Rhyme

Overture

Watch how your child enjoys saying particular words. She will have favorites. Her speech will become more modulated and articulate as she nears her fifth birthday. Tongue twisters are often very enjoyable for preschoolers.

Performance

Play: To help your four-year-old learn to say difficult words, recite tongue twisters.
What you will need: No special equipment is needed for this game.
How to play: Teach your child the rhyme, "Peter, Peter, Pumpkin-Eater,"
   Peter, Peter, pumpkin-eater
   Had a wife and couldn't keep her.
   Put her in a pumpkin shell,
   And there he kept her very well.

Finale

To really challenge your four-year-old's pronunciation, teach her "Peter Piper Picked a Peck of Pickled Peppers."
   Peter Piper picked a peck of pickled peppers.
   A peck of pickled peppers, Peter Piper picked.
   If Peter Piper picked a peck of pickled peppers,
   Where's the peck of pickled peppers Peter Piper picked?

Encore

Create special tongue twisters using your child's name and favorite toys, foods, or games.
Example:
   Clever Kurt, kitchen cleaner,
   Loved to keep the kitchen neater.
   Clever Kurt mopped the hall,
   Clever Kurt washed the wall.
   Clever Kurt, kitchen cleaner
   Loved to clean, mop, and wash it all.
Or,
   Bernadette bopped a big baseball
   Back and forth, back and forth.
   If Bernadette bopped a big baseball
   Back and forth, back and forth,
   Where's the big baseball Bernadette bopped?

Crooked Sixpence

An old woman was sweeping her house,
and she found a little crooked sixpence.

Overture

Watch your child's face when you are reading a story to him. You will see by his eyes when he is anticipating the next event.

Performance

Play: To encourage your preschooler to participate in the telling of a long, repetitive story, share the story "Crooked Sixpence."

What you will need: No special equipment is needed to act out this rhyme.

How to play: Begin by telling the whole story to your child. When you tell the story a second time, pause to see if your child can fill in the last word(s) of each repetitive sentence.

An old woman was sweeping her house, and she found a little crooked sixpence. "What," said she, "shall I do with this little sixpence? I will go to market and buy a little pig."

As she was coming home, she came to a stile, but the piggy would not go over the stile. So she said to the pig, "Get over the stile or I shan't get home tonight." But the pig would not.

She went a little farther, and she met a dog. So she said to the dog, "Dog, dog, bite pig. Piggy won't get over the stile, and I shan't get home tonight." But the dog would not.

So she walked a little farther, and she met a stick. So she said, "Stick, stick, beat dog. Dog won't bite pig. Piggy won't get over the stile, and I shan't get home tonight." But the stick would not.

So she walked a little farther, and she met a fire. So she said, "Fire, fire, burn stick. Stick won't beat dog. Dog won't bite pig. Piggy won't get over the stile, and I shan't get home tonight." But the fire would not.

So she walked a little farther, and she met some water. She said, "Water, water, quench fire. Fire won't burn stick. Stick won't beat dog. Dog won't bite pig. Piggy won't get over the stile, and I shan't get home tonight." But the water would not.

So she walked a little farther, and she met an ox. She said, "Ox, ox, drink water. Water won't quench fire. Fire won't burn stick. Stick won't beat dog. Dog won't bite pig. Piggy won't get over the stile, and I shan't get home tonight."

And the ox said, "If you will go to the yonder hay makers, and fetch me a wisp of hay, I'll drink the water."

So away the old woman went to the hay makers, and said, "Hay makers, give me a wisp of hay. Ox won't drink water. Water won't quench fire. Fire won't burn stick. Stick won't beat dog. Dog won't bite pig. Piggy won't get over the stile, and I shan't get home tonight."

The hay makers said to her, "If you will go to yonder stream, and fetch us a bucket of water, we will give you the hay." So away the old woman went; but when she got to the stream, she found the bucket was full of holes. So she covered the bottom with pebbles, and then filled the bucket with water, and away she went, carrying it to the hay makers. Then they gave her a wisp of hay.

As soon as the ox had eaten the hay, he began to drink the water. The water began to quench the fire. The fire began to burn the stick. The stick began to beat the dog. The dog began to bite the pig. The little pig in a fright jumped over the stile. And so the old woman got home that night.

Finale

If possible, read picture books that have repetitive texts to your child. A children's librarian can recommend appropriate titles, if suggestions are needed.

           © Instructional Fair • TS Denison

Little Miss Muffet

Little Miss Muffet sat on a tuffet,
Eating her curds and whey.
There came a spider,
And sat down beside her,
And frightened Miss Muffet away.
—Traditional Rhyme

Overture

Listen, and you may hear your child talking to herself or an imaginary person. Four-year-olds talk all day, even when there is no one there to listen.

Performance

Play: To encourage your four-year-old to make up dialogue to perform impromptu plays, turn "Little Miss Muffet" into a one-act play.

What you will need: Plastic bowl, wooden spoon, big pillow

How to play: Recite the rhyme for your child. Then have her act it out as you recite it.

Example:

Little Miss Muffet (*Enter the room with a bowl.*)
Sat on a tuffet, (*Sit down on the pillow and stir.*)
Eating her curds and whey. (*Pretend to eat from the bowl.*)
There came a spider, (*Pretend to see a spider.*)
And sat down beside her, (*Pretend the spider is coming closer.*)
And frightened Miss Muffet away. (*Drop bowl and spoon and run away.*)

Next have your child make up dialogue that tells what she is doing.

Example:

Enters and says, "Hi, I am Little Miss Muffet."
Sits down and says, "This is my tuffet."
Stirs and says, "These are my curds and whey."
Spots the spider, acts afraid, and says, "Oh, dear, look at that spider!"
Watches the spider and says, "Oh my! It is going to bite me."
Runs off, saying, "I must run away before that spider gets me."

Finale

Another good nursery rhyme for you and your child to perform as an impromptu play is "Jack and Jill Went Up the Hill." Encourage your child to make up the dialogue and actions.

Jack and Jill went up the hill,
To fetch a pail of water.
Jack fell down and broke his crown,
And Jill came tumbling after.

Encore

"Little Bo-Peep" is yet another excellent nursery rhyme that can be turned into a little play.

Little Bo-Peep has lost her sheep,
And can't tell where to find them.
Let them alone, and they'll come home,
Wagging their tails behind them.

What Would You Do?

Oh, what would you do, if you had to eat a rock?
What would you do if a bumblebee was in your sock,
If a turtle snapped at your toes, or a rose grew out of your nose?
Oh, what would you do, what would you do?

Overture

Four-year-olds like to talk about imaginary things. Motivate your child's language acquisition by playing "What Would You Do?"

Performance

Play: To encourage your preschooler to use language to talk about imaginary situations, play "What Would You Do?"

What you will need: No special equipment is needed to play this game.

How to play: Ask silly questions to challenge your child's imagination. Praise all of his creative ideas.

Examples: What would you do . . .

- ◆ if you had to eat a rock?
- ◆ if a turtle snapped at your toes?
- ◆ if root beer came out of the kitchen faucet?
- ◆ if the sky turned orange?
- ◆ if your arms and legs were made of rubber?

- ◆ if a bumblebee was in your sock?
- ◆ if a rose grew out of your nose?
- ◆ if it rained pancakes?
- ◆ if you woke up and you were a giant?

Finale

Another variation of this game is to ask "How Would You Feel?"

Examples: How would you feel . . .

- ◆ if a new person moved in next door that looked exactly like you?
- ◆ if your skin turned purple and stayed that way?
- ◆ if every time it rained you had to stay inside your home because you were chocolate and getting wet would melt you?
- ◆ if you could only meow like a cat for a whole day?
- ◆ if your name was Snicklefrizzel Bartholomew Redrickoo Boomerang Man?
- ◆ if you could understand what animals were thinking?

Encore

After playing "What Would You Do?" or "How Would You Feel?" have your child draw pictures about the stories.

Challenge your child by asking questions and having him act out the answers.

- ◆ How would it be if you were a bird and could fly?
- ◆ How would it be if you were a big race horse and could gallop fast?
- ◆ How would it be if you were a snake and slithered along the ground?

        © Instructional Fair • TS Denison

How?

Mary, Mary, quite contrary,
How does your garden grow? . . .
—Traditional Rhyme

Overture

As much as a two-year-old loves to ask "Why?" a four-year-old's favorite question is "How?" When a two-year-old asks a question, usually she wants to get attention, but more often than not, when a four-year-old asks a question she wants to know the answer. Take seriously all of your child's questions. Watch how your child will listen to an answer if it is simple and direct.

Performance

Play: To encourage your child's curiosity, try to answer all of her questions that begin with "How?"

What you will need: No special equipment is needed for this activity.

How to play: When answering the question "How?" keep your explanation simple and accurate. Often a child this age does not expect details, but rather a general answer. Use correct vocabulary for body parts, tools, etc. When your child asks you a question and you do not know the answer, seize the opportunity to go to the library or use a reference book to find out more about the new topic. Following are descriptions of two books that every child will enjoy "reading." The books answer hundreds of questions your child may have about how nature and machines work.

Finale

How Nature Works by David Burnie (Reader's Digest, 1991) gives one-hundred ways parents and children can share the secrets of nature. The beautiful photographs show fascinating things such as how a toad spots, attacks, and catches its prey with its long sticky tongue. Chapters include: Looking at Life (cells, natural selection, classifying, plants); The World of Plants and Fungi (how plants make food, structure of flowers, seeds, germination, trees, fungi); Life in the Water (lake, stream, pond, and seashore life); Insects and Other Invertebrates (insects, grasshoppers, butterflies, moths, ants, bees, earthworms); Birds (flight, wings, feathers, eggs, nests); Reptiles (snakes, crocodiles, alligators, lizards, turtles); Mammals (skeletons, teeth, vision, hearing, living by night, tracks, feeding). There is a wealth of knowledge in this book and it will be a resource your child will refer to many times.

Encore

David Macaulay's *The Way Things Work* (Houghton Mifflin Company, 1988) contains chapters on Mechanics of Movement (inclined planes, levers, wheels and axles, gears and belts, cams and cranks, pulleys, springs); Harnessing the Elements (flotation, flying, pressure power, exploiting heat); Working with Waves (light and images, photography, printing, sound and music, telecommunications); and Electricity & Automation (photocopier, ionizer, solar cell, magnetism, computers). The cartoon-type illustrations take children through step-by-step explanations. Just looking at the pictures will give your child a wealth of scientific knowledge.

Name the Ways

. . . Then as evening gave way to the shadows of night,
Their watchman, the glowworm came out with his light. . . .
—Traditional Rhyme

Overture

When your child was two- and three-years old, he began to notice the similarities and differences between objects. Listen, now that his language skills are developing, he will be able to verbalize these similarities and differences.

Performance

Play: To help your child verbalize the similarities and differences between two things, play "Name the Ways."

What you will need: Fruit or pictures of fruit (such as apple, orange, banana, kiwi, lime), vegetables (such as carrot, green onion, eggplant), basket

How to play: Place all the foods in a basket on the table where your child can see and reach them. Place two foods on the table side by side. Ask your child to name a way they are alike. Then have him name a way they are not alike. There are many correct answers for each example.

Examples	Alike	Different
◆ apple/orange	shape—round	color—red/orange
◆ carrot/banana	shape—long pointy	type—vegetable/fruit
◆ green onion/kiwi	color—green	type—vegetable/fruit
◆ eggplant/apple	texture—smooth	color—purple/red
◆ orange/banana	type—fruit	texture—bumpy/smooth
◆ lime/kiwi	shape—oval	texture—smooth/fuzzy

Finale

Have your child compare and contrast, naming as many similarities and differences as possible. Stimulating your child's thinking and challenging his vocabulary will give his thinking skills a big boost.

Example: Teddy bear and book

Similarities	Differences
◆ Both are toys.	◆ One is roundish and one is square.
◆ Both belong to the child.	◆ One is thick and one is thin.
◆ Both belong in the child's bedroom.	◆ One is soft and one is hard.
◆ Both can be held.	◆ One is fuzzy and one is smooth.
◆ Neither is to be left out in the rain.	

Encore

Another game to teach the verbalizing of similarities and differences is to name an object in the room. Then ask your child to look around the room and name something that is the same shape, color, size, or texture, etc., as the object you named.

   © Instructional Fair • TS Denison

How Many Fish?

One, two, three, four, five,
Catching fishes all alive.
Why did you let them go?
Because they bit my finger so.
Which finger did they bite?
The little finger on the right.
—Traditional Rhyme

Overture

Listen to your four-year-old's speech patterns, and you may discover that she has mastered some basic rules of grammar.

Performance

Play: To help your four-year-old understand that "is" is used for one object and "are" is used for more than one, play "How Many Fish?"

What you will need: Yardstick, meterstick, or a branch about the same length, string, five large paper fish cut from construction paper, hole punch, large paper clip

How to play: Use the hole punch to punch a hole in each fish. Bend a large paper clip into a hook. Tie the stick to one end of the string and the hook to the other end to resemble a fishing pole. Sit on the floor behind a large sofa or chair. Your child is to "go fishing" by hanging the fishing hook over the edge of the chair or sofa. Put one or more fish on the end of her pole and tug it so she can "reel" them in. Ask her, "How many fish did you catch?" Emphasize:

◆ One fish "is" on the line.
◆ Two (three, four, five) fishes "are" on the line.

Finale

Another way of teaching "is" and "are" is to use magazine pictures of people. Cut out a variety of pictures of people. Hold up a picture and ask questions that can be answered: "He 'is'," "She 'is'," or "They 'are'."

Examples:

◆ Who in this picture are children? (They are.)
◆ Who in this picture is a doctor? (She is.)
◆ Who in this picture is wearing a red hat? (He is.)

Encore

On other occasions, ask questions about daily routines that can be answered with "He is," "She is," or "They are."

Examples:

◆ Who is at school? (They are.)
◆ Who is at work? (She is.)
◆ Who is here in the house? (We are.)

When?

When Jacky's a very good boy,
He shall have cakes and a custard; . . .
—Traditional Rhyme

Overture

At four years of age, your child has a much clearer sense of the times: "yesterday," "today," and "tomorrow." Listen to see if he speaks in the correct tense when talking about the past, present, or future. With practice your preschooler can master speaking in tenses.

Performance

Play: To introduce and reinforce the use of past, present, and future tenses, play "When?"
What you will need: No special equipment is needed to play this game.
How to play: Simply ask your child questions that can be answered using a past, present, or future tense. Then when he tells you the correct day, put it into a sentence including the appropriate tense. Example:

◆ When did we go to the circus? (Yesterday, we "went" to the circus.)
◆ When are we going to the birthday party? (Tomorrow, we "will go" to the party.)
◆ When shall we have lunch? (We "are going" to eat lunch now.)
◆ When will we go to bed? (Tonight, we "will go" to bed.)

Finale

Some tenses you can model for your child include:

Past	Present	Future
Ate	Eat	Will eat
Drove	Drive	Will drive
Jumped	Jump	Will jump
Rode	Ride	Will ride
Talked	Talk	Will talk
Went	Go	Will go

Encore

When your child uses incorrect grammer, do not correct him or ask him to say it correctly. Instead, simply model the correct way to say the sentence.

© Instructional Fair • TS Denison

Super Star

Little Nancy Etticote, in a white petticoat.
With a warm glow and a red nose.
The longer she stands, the shorter she grows. (Candle)
—Traditional Rhyme

CHILD'S NAME HERE

Overture

Two- and three-year-olds know their first names but by age four, many children know their middle and last names, too. If your child does not know her last name, begin teaching it to her.

Performance

Play: To help your child practice pronouncing her middle and last names as well as her first, play "Super Star."
What you will need: Large cardboard star shape, glitter glue, black marker
How to play: Write your child's full name in the center of the big star. Let her use the marker to trace the letters. Show her how to decorate the points on the star using glitter glue. Hang the Super Star name tag on her bedroom door. Ask her at different times to tell you her full name.

Finale

Use family photograph albums to teach your four-year-old the full names of family members. As you look at each photograph, give the person's full name. Ask your child to repeat the name. Then go back, and look at the album again and see how many of the names your child can remember.

Encore

Just for fun, give full names to your family pets. If your family's last name is Brown, instead of calling the family dog "Buster," call him "Buster Bradley Brown." Have your child invent middle and last names for all of her stuffed toys. Make miniature star-shaped name tags for the stuffed animals. Punch a hole in each one and string yarn through the hole. Hang the name tags on the stuffed animals.

Where Do You Live?

Wee Willie Winkie runs through the town,
Upstairs and downstairs, in his nightgown;
Rapping at the window, crying at the lock,
"Are the children in their beds, for now it's ten o'clock!"
—Traditional Rhyme

Overture

Four-year-olds need to know how to tell adults where they live. In case you and your child are separated, it is important that she be able to tell an adult where she lives.

Performance

Play: To encourage your child to memorize her address, play "Where Do You Live?"
What you will need: Old letters with envelopes, cardboard signs with your house number and the name of your street written on them, cloth bag with a strap for carrying mail

How to play: Hang the street sign and house number up where your child can see them. Put a bunch of old mail in a cloth bag and put the strap over your shoulder. Pretend to be the mail carrier delivering mail to your child. Ask, "Is this (say your address)?" If the child says "Yes," give her some letters. Sometimes give the wrong house number or street name. Do not deliver mail to the wrong address. Take turns being the mail carrier.

Finale

Use shoe boxes to play another mail delivery game. Write a different numeral on each box. Write matching numerals on pieces of old mail. Have your child "deliver" the mail to the right addresses by placing the letters in the appropriate shoe boxes.

Encore

Go outside to look at the numbers on your house. Walk to the corner and look at your street sign. Have your child "read" the numbers and name of the street. When visiting other neighborhoods, read the street signs and house numbers where friends and grandparents live, too.

        © Instructional Fair • TS Denison

How Many Ways?

How many days has my baby to play?
Saturday, Sunday, Monday,
Tuesday, Wednesday, Thursday, Friday,
Saturday, Sunday, Monday.
—Traditional Rhyme

Overture

Watch, and you will notice that your preschooler will move back and forth freely between fantasy and reality. Ask him a make-believe question and he will most likely be willing to give you a fanciful answer.

Performance

Play: To help your child think in creative ways, play "How Many Ways?"

What you will need: No special equipment is needed to play this game.

How to play: Ask the following questions. Make lists of answers.

- ◆ How many different desserts can we make with apples?
- ◆ How many ways can you dance?
- ◆ How many ways can you climb a tree?
- ◆ How many ways can you play in the bathtub?
- ◆ How many ways can you tell someone you like her?

Finale

Use the same technique of asking questions to have your child think in more fanciful ways by giving your child "make-believe story starters." Some examples include:

- ◆ Tell a story about building a stairway to the clouds.
- ◆ Tell a story about a fairy who paints a rainbow in the sky.
- ◆ Tell a story about a bird that can fly backward.
- ◆ Tell a story about a man who can talk to fish.
- ◆ Tell a story about a little boy who can pick up heavy things like school buses.
- ◆ Tell a story about a little girl who can understand the thoughts of butterflies.

Encore

On other occasions, have your child invent the questions instead of the answers. Then, together make up stories to answer the questions.

Sing a Song

Little Tommy Tucker,
Sings for his supper. . . .
—Traditional Rhyme

Overture

Four-year-olds just love to listen to themselves talk. They chatter all day long. Channel some of this energy into a project. Have your preschooler make audiotapes. Date each tape, and put them away for safe keeping. Listen to them in a month or two.

Performance

Play: To give your preschooler an opportunity to hear himself talk, use a tape recorder to record his dialogue.

What you will need: Tape recorder, microphone, blank audiotape

How to play: Ask your preschooler to make a tape of all the songs he knows. Encourage him to sing familiar songs like "Happy Birthday," "Jingle Bells," and "Row, Row, Row Your Boat." Also refer to page 129, 130 and 133 for simple rhymes and songs.

Finale

Have your four-year-old make a tape of tongue twisters. See ideas on page 131. Include saying any of the following three times in a row as quickly as he can:

◆ Hickery, dickery, dock; the mouse ran up the clock.
◆ Pease porridge hot, pease porridge cold, pease porridge in the pot nine days old.
◆ Hey diddle, diddle, the cat and the fiddle.
◆ Cock-a-doodle-doo. My dame has lost her shoe.
◆ Charley Wag, Charley Wag, ate the pudding and left the bag.
◆ Rain, rain, go to Spain, don't come back again.
◆ Wooley Foster has gone to sea, with silver buckles on his knees.
◆ Bryan O'Lin had no breeches to wear, so he bought him a sheepskin and made him a pair.

Encore

Invite your child to tell stories and make tapes of them, too. Use some of the make-believe story starters on page 141. After your child makes a tape, listen to it together. Send it to relatives who live in other states so they can hear how many new words your child can speak.

© Instructional Fair • TS Denison

Keeping Track

Milestone	Date	Comments
Can follow directions that include adverbs		
Can recite some nursery rhymes from memory		
Can remember the words and sing songs		
Can recite some tongue twisters		
Can participate in the telling of repetitive stories		
Can make up dialogue and perform plays		
Can speak of imaginary situations		
Can grasp explanations of how things work		
Can verbalize similarities and differences		
Sometimes uses correct grammar		
Can use past, present, and future tenses		
Can state full name and age		
Can state home address		
Can use language to think creatively		
Can make tapes of songs, tongue twisters, and stories		

Flights of Fancy

Creative/Imaginative Development

Contemplate

Something magical happens when a child turns four. Suddenly she is aware of what is "good" and what is "bad." Children at this age love to hear stories about real people, especially members of their families. They enjoy hearing about how "good" or how "bad" their parents were when they were little. Most four-year-olds have a fascination for what their parents were like when they were children.

Teachers and artists agree that children are best encouraged in their creativity if they are permitted as much freedom as possible. You will do best by enjoying and permitting your child's own enjoyment of a large variety of artwork. Encourage your child to work in as many craft mediums as possible.

Four-year-olds create to please themselves, but they also like to please those around them. When you admire and praise your child's work, it motivates your child to create other things. As you lavish her with praise, the more likely she is to feel free and inspired in her creativity. However, keep in mind that too much praise may make the child try to please the adult instead of creating for her own enjoyment.

Some children show their creativity not in works of art, but in their creative play. Music, puppets, and costumes provide stimulation for creative play. Use the games and activities in this chapter to foster creativity in art, musical experiences, and dramatic play.

Creative/Imaginative Milestones: Four Years

- ◆ Will be able to tell and understand jokes
- ◆ Will be inventive in fantasy play
- ◆ Will enjoy pantomiming
- ◆ Will use large objects as props in fantasy play
- ◆ Will enjoy pantomiming animals
- ◆ Will enjoy providing sound effects for stories
- ◆ Will enjoy dressing up in grown-up clothes
- ◆ Will enjoy watching and using puppets
- ◆ Will enjoy crafts with paints
- ◆ Will enjoy crafts with clay
- ◆ Will enjoy crafts with paper
- ◆ Will enjoy cutting and pasting

General Tips

Four-year-olds are sometimes difficult to handle. They have emotional highs and lows that boomerang them from self-confident to insecure and back again. Often children this age resent changes in daily routines because it makes them feel insecure—they are afraid they will not know what to do.

Make-believe play is a way for a child this age to work out all of her doubts and fears about the world around her. You can enrich your child's world and help her feel more self-confident by encouraging her fanciful, imaginary games. Costumes, such as dress-up clothes and fairy-tale character costumes, are especially fun for preschoolers.

Any make-believe situation you present to your child will be appreciated. For example: give a four-year-old a chopstick and play classical music and in a second her will be leading the orchestra. Background music will add to the pleasure of her fantasy games.

Appropriate toys for encouraging a four-year-old's fantasy play include:
- Props such as costumes and dress-up clothes
- Props such as magic wands, batons, cash registers, play telephones
- Full-length mirror
- Child-sized playhouse, dishes, table, chairs, etc.
- Child-sized forts, treehouses, etc.
- Tape player and instrumental music
- Child-sized musical instruments
- Place that can be used as a stage
- Puppets, puppet stage
- Paints—all types, paintbrushes, large art paper
- Play clay, molding materials
- Variety of papers, including construction and tissue paper
- Glue sticks, glitter, stickers, adhesive stars, scraps of fabric
- Blunt-tip scissors

Elephant Jokes

How do you know if an elephant is hiding in your closet?
Because you'll smell the peanuts on his breath.

Overture

Four-year-olds not only have a sense of humor, they enjoy laughing tremendously. They appreciate humor and like to kid around. Watch your child's face when you joke with him, and you may see anything from a loud laugh to a subtle giggle or amused sigh. A four-year-old's face runs the gamut of humorous expressions. Preschoolers especially enjoy exaggeration, nonsense rhymes, and humor.

Performance

Play: To encourage your child to tell jokes, tell him some silly elephant jokes.
What you will need: Nothing is needed for this activity.
How to play: Ask your four-year-old a silly elephant riddle. Praise all of his answers. Remember, the answers given are not the only possible answers. What your child thinks of will be just as funny.

- How can you tell if an elephant's been sleeping in your bed?
  Because you'll feel all the empty peanut shells in the sheets.
- How can you tell if an elephant has been playing on your computer?
  Because you'll see the peanut butter stains on the keyboard.
- How do you stop an elephant from slipping through the eye of a needle?
  Tie a knot in its tail.
- How do you stop an elephant from slipping down the drain in the bathtub?
  Tie a knot in its trunk.
- Why do elephants paint the bottoms of their feet yellow?
  So they can hide upside down in banana cream pies. You've never found an elephant in your banana cream pie have you? No? Works then, doesn't it.

Finale

On another occasion, ask your child some other elephant jokes.
- Why do elephants wear sandals to the beach?
  To stop their feet from sinking into the sand
- Why do ostriches bury their heads in the sand?
  To watch all the elephants who didn't wear sandals to the beach
- Why do elephants wear sunglasses to the movies?
  So no one will ask them for their autographs
- And why do they wear sunglasses to the beach?
  To keep the sun out of their eyes, of course
- Why do some elephants wear red nail polish?
  So they can hide in a strawberry patch
- Why are goldfish orange and elephants gray?
  So you can tell them from bluebirds
- What goes clomp, clomp, clomp, squish, clomp, clomp, clomp, squish?
  An elephant with one wet sneaker

Encore

When telling jokes, ask your child to explain why the joke is funny.

146

© Instructional Fair • TS Denison

Dancing Hands

Handy Spandy, Jack a-dandy,
Loves plum-cake and sugar candy.
One hand up, one hand down,
Out he comes, hop, hop, hop.

Overture

Four-year-olds are inventive and fanciful in their play. Watch, and will may notice how your child will independently find props and tools to make his games more imaginative. You can stimulate his imagination by providing a variety of stages for his fantasy play.

Performance

Play: To give your child an opportunity to be inventive in fantasy, play "Dancing Hands."
What you will need: Large cardboard box (big enough for your child to sit inside), audiotape or CD of music
How to play: Use a straight edge to cut two 12 inch (31 cm) diameter holes in three sides and the top of the box. Set the box on its side so the flaps form a door. Have your child go inside the box and close the flaps. Play the music. The object of the game is for your child to stick his hands out of the different holes and move them to the music.

Finale

Try a variety of different kinds of music with the box. Suggest that instead of dancing hands, your child can stick out other body parts and move them to music, including:
   ◆ Feet
   ◆ Elbows
   ◆ Knees
   ◆ One finger or thumb
   ◆ Toes
   ◆ Hair

Encore

Also try covering your child's crouched body with things besides a box and invite him to move to the music. Examples:
   ◆ Lightweight blanket
   ◆ Bed sheet
   ◆ Lightweight plastic tablecloth
   ◆ Large strip of gauze
   ◆ Silk scarves

Circus Acts

Ride a cock-horse to Banbury Cross,
To see a fine lady upon a white horse.
With rings on her fingers and bells on her toes,
She shall have music wherever she goes.
—Traditional Rhyme

Overture

Pantomiming is a good way to engage a four-year-old's imagination. Sometimes, leading your child's fantasy play will enrich her games. After you suggest a certain kind of play, to get her to use her imagination, step aside and let her take the lead.

Performance

Play: To encourage your child to pantomime, begin by having her pretend she is walking a tightrope.
What you will need: Chalk line 10' to 12' (3–3.6 m) long
How to play: Tell your child to pretend that the chalk line is a tightrope. She is to walk the tightrope by placing one foot in front of the other as she walks on the imaginary rope. Suggest that your child hold her arms out to the sides to help her balance.

Finale

Clowning is another circus act that four-year-olds enjoy pantomiming. Before clowning, paint your child's face like a clown. Explain to your child that clowns convey stories without speaking. Have your child try to pantomime some of the following:
- Walking a tightrope using an umbrella for balance
- Throwing a bucket of water on another clown
- Riding a unicycle
- Juggling water balloons that break
- Eating sour pickles or hot spaghetti
- Walking barefoot on ice
- Getting trapped inside a clear, plastic box
- Inflating a huge balloon by blowing into it, then getting lifted off the ground by the balloon

Encore

Other circus acts to pantomime include:
- Juggler
- Trapeze artist
- Lion/bear tamer
- Lion jumping through a fiery hoop
- Dancing bear
- Fire-eater
- Bareback riding
- Ringmaster
- Dressed up dog dancing

        © Instructional Fair • TS Denison

Billy Goats Gruff

"Don't eat me," said the littlest Billy Goat Gruff.
"Soon my big brother will be here,
and he is much bigger and tastier than me."
—"Three Billy Goats Gruff"

Overture

Fairy tales are good beginnings for make-believe play. After reading a fairy tale to your child, do an impromptu acting of some of the scenes. Watch and see how creative she can be.

Performance

Play: To encourage your four-year-old to pretend that large playground equipment is part of a fantasy game, play "Billy Goats Gruff."

What you will need: Slide (bed, big box, etc.)

How to play: Begin by reading the story "The Three Billy Goats Gruff" to your child. Then pretend to be the troll and hide under the "bridge" which could be a slide (bed, big box, etc.). As your child slides down the slide (crawls over the bed, around the box, etc.), try to touch her fingers or toes. When she gets to the bottom of the slide, block her way and say that you are Mr. Troll. The object is for her to talk her way out of it. ("Please don't eat me. I am too little. I won't make a good meal. Wait for my bigger brother who is coming along soon.") On the second time down the slide, let her be the middle-sized Billy Goat Gruff; the third time she can be the Big Billy Goat Gruff, etc.

Finale

Use large playground equipment as the setting for fairy tale plays or other classic stories. Use the jungle gym to be Grandmother's house in "Little Red Riding Hood," the home of the third little pig in "The Three Little Pigs," or the bridge in "The Three Billy Goats Gruff."

Encore

Read a variety of fairy tales to your child and follow up with make-believe play. Try some of these:
- ◆ "The Three Bears"
- ◆ "The Three Little Pigs"
- ◆ "The Gingerbread Man"
- ◆ "Little Red Riding Hood"
- ◆ "The Ugly Duckling"

The House That Jack Built

This is the house that Jack built
This is the malt that lay in the house that Jack built.

Overture..

Four-year-olds often enjoy participating in stories they hear. Watch your child as you read a familiar story; you may see him mouthing some of the words with you.

Performance..

Play: To give your child the opportunity to provide sound effects for a story as it is read, use the story "The House That Jack Built."

What you will need: No special equipment is needed for this activity.

How to play: Read the following story to your child.

This is the house that Jack built.

This is the malt, that lay in the house that Jack built.

This is the rat, that ate the malt, that lay in the house that Jack built.

This is the cat, that killed the rat, that ate the malt, that lay in the house that Jack built.

This is the dog, that worried the cat, that killed the rat, that ate the malt, that lay in the house that Jack built.

This is the cow with the crumpled horn, that tossed the dog, that worried the cat, that killed the rat, that ate the malt, that lay in the house that Jack built.

This is the maiden all forlorn, that milk'd the cow with the crumpled horn, that tossed the dog, that worried the cat, that killed the rat, that ate the malt, that lay in the house that Jack built.

This is the man all tatter'd and torn, that kiss'd the maiden all forlorn, that milk'd the cow with the crumpled horn, that tossed the dog, that worried the cat, that killed the rat, that ate the malt, that lay in the house that Jack built.

This is the priest all shaven and shorn, that married the man all tatter'd and torn, that kiss'd the maiden all forlorn, that milk'd the cow with the crumpled horn, that tossed the dog, that worried the cat, that killed the rat, that ate the malt, that lay in the house that Jack built.

This is the cock that crow'd in the morn, that waked the priest all shaven and shorn, that married the man all tatter'd and torn, that kiss'd the maiden all forlorn, that milk'd the cow with the crumpled horn, that tossed the dog, that worried the cat, that killed the rat, that ate the malt, that lay in the house that Jack built.

This is the farmer who sow'd the corn, that kept the cock that crow'd in the morn, that waked the priest all shaven and shorn, that married the man all tatter'd and torn, that kiss'd the maiden all forlorn, that milk'd the cow with the crumpled horn, that tossed the dog, that worried the cat, that killed the rat, that ate the malt, that lay in the house that Jack built.

The House That Jack Built, Cont.

Finale

Recite the story again. This time substitute certain sounds for animals or people.
Examples:

- ◆ Jack built—Ratt-a-tat-tat (hammer)
- ◆ Malt—Yum, yum
- ◆ Rat—Squeak, squeak
- ◆ Cat—Meow, meow
- ◆ Dog—Bark, bark
- ◆ Cow—Moo, moo
- ◆ Maiden—Give a big "sigh."
- ◆ Man—Shout "Hurrah."
- ◆ Priest—Say, "Let us pray."
- ◆ Cock—Cock-a-doodle-doo
- ◆ Farmer—Say, "This story is almost through."

Encore

After your child learns the story, recite it again. Encourage your child to change the story by featuring different animals or people.

        151

It's a Zoo

Bossy-cow, bossy-cow, where do you lie?
In the green meadow under the sky. . . .
—Traditional Rhyme

Overture

Four-year-olds enjoy observing animals. Watch your child the next time you visit a zoo, pet store, neighborhood park, or humane society to discover which animals are his favorites.

Performance

Play: To encourage your child to pretend to be a variety of animals, play "It's a Zoo."
What you will need: No special equipment is needed to play this game.
How to play: Use pantomimes of different animals to stimulate your child's imagination. Demonstrate and describe the way an animal moves, then have your child pretend to be that animal. Try some of these:

- ◆ Cow grazing and eating grass
- ◆ Butterfly emerging from its cocoon
- ◆ Turtle waking up, sticking out its head, and slowly walking away
- ◆ Chick hatching from an egg
- ◆ Caterpillar spinning itself into a cocoon
- ◆ Spider spinning a web
- ◆ Baby bird learning to fly
- ◆ A snake slithering across wet grass
- ◆ A rabbit coming up out of a hole
- ◆ A beaver knawing down a tree
- ◆ A caterpillar or bug creeping up a tree or along a branch
- ◆ A puppy playing with a shoe

Finale

Recite the rhyme while your child pantomimes the movements.
Bossy-cow, bossy-cow, where do you lie?
In the green meadow under the sky.
Billy-horse, billy-horse, where do you lie?
Out in the stable with nobody nigh.
Birdies bright, birdies sweet, where do you lie?
Up in the treetops—oh, ever so high!
Baby dear, baby love, where do you lie?
In my warm crib, with Mamma close by.

Encore

Also use the rhyme as a memory verse. Read the questions, and see if your child can answer.

© Instructional Fair • TS Denison

Having a Party

Sing song! Merry-go-round,
Here we go up to the moon, Oh!

Overture

Any excuse for a party will be welcomed by your preschooler. Finding a penny, seeing the first star, learning something new—anything you can imagine is a good reason to celebrate. Watch your child when you mention having a party and she will probably have suggestions for making the occasion even more festive.

Performance

Play: To encourage your preschooler to dress up in grown-up clothes, have a pretend party.
What you will need: Fancy, old dress-up clothes such as a bridal or evening gown, suit jacket, tie, veil, hat, gloves, etc.
How to play: Have your child use some dress-up clothes to get as fancy as possible. Then put on some ballroom music and dance. You might pretend it is Cinderella's ball, a birthday party for Sleeping Beauty or a superhero, and so on.

Finale

Big hats are extremely motivating for preschoolers. Have your child help you create wonderful hats that she can use for dress-up play.

- ◆ Grocery Bag Derby—Roll edges of a paper bag down until it looks like a derby. Decorate with silk flowers, feathers, etc.
- ◆ Paper Plate Hats—Use a hole punch to punch a hole in either side of a large, sturdy paper plate. Decorate with large plastic flowers. Thread ribbon through both holes and tie under the chin.
- ◆ Paper Bowl Hats—Choose paper bowls that fit on your child's head. Paint and decorate with stickers, glitter, ribbons, etc.

Encore

Providing a box of dress-up clothes and interesting props will encourage your child's fantasy play. See more ideas on page 145, too.

Puppet Plays

Punch and Judy fought for a pie,
Punch gave Judy a knock in the eye.
Says Punch to Judy, "Will you have any more?"
Says Judy to Punch, "My eyes are too sore."
—Traditional Rhyme

Overture

Observe your four-year-old as he watches a puppet show. He will more than likely want to talk to the puppet and will, of course, answer any questions the puppet may ask him.

Performance

Play: To encourage your child to use puppets for play, suggest using simple stories like "The Three Little Pigs" or "The Three Bears" as stories for the puppet shows.

What you will need: Paper plates, craft sticks, scissors, watercolor markers, glue

How to play: Tell your child the story. Use pig or bear stick puppets to add dialogue to the storytelling. Then encourage your child to use the puppets to retell the story. Paper plate puppets with craft stick handles are easy to make.

Finale

Another good puppet play to perform with a pig puppet is "This Little Piggie." Your child holds up the puppet each time you say a line of the poem.

This little piggie went to market.
This little piggie stayed home.
This little piggie had roast meat.
This little piggie had none.
And this little piggie cried, "Wee, wee, wee, I can't find my way home."

Encore

You and your child can make sock puppets, too. Cut facial features out of felt scraps and glue them onto old socks to create snakes, worms, etc. To make a puppet stage for your child's play, all you will need is a large cardboard box and a utility knife. Turn the large cardboard box on its side so the flaps are the back of the stage. Cut out an opening at the top of the front of the box as illustrated. The puppeteer sits inside the box and holds his hands up so the puppets are seen in the window.

© Instructional Fair • TS Denison

Dancing Fingers

Dance, little fingers, dance.
Dance, ye merrymen, everyone.
Dance, thumbkin, dance.
Thumbkin, he can dance alone.

Overture

Music and crafts naturally go together for children at this age. Both art and music set free the creative spirit in children. Watch to see if your child enjoys listening to music while she is doing craft projects.

Performance

Play: To provide your preschooler with creative crafts, use an assortment of paints.

What you will need: Newspapers, finger paints, large sheets of finger paint paper, music on audiotape or CD

How to play: Cover the work surface with newspapers. Wet the paper slightly and place it on a flat surface. Put a few spoonfuls of paint on the paper. Begin to play the music. Encourage your child to spread her fingers in the paint and move them around to the music. If the paint gets a little dry, add a few drops of water. Try other music with different colors. Save the pictures, and label them with the type of music that inspired the work.

Finale

When finger painting, try some varied ways of moving the color on the paper including:
◆ Swirl paint with a comb and other interesting kitchen gadgets.
◆ Control color flow with a cotton swab.
◆ Place a blank sheet of paper on top of a finger painting and press down to make a print of the original.
◆ Use a plastic fork or spoon to swirl in a second color.
◆ While the paint is still wet, sprinkle with glitter.

Encore

If you want to make your own finger paint, soap paint, or squeeze bottle paint, follow the recipes below.

Finger Paint—Mix 2 cups (474 ml) liquid laundry starch with 1 cup (237 ml) powdered tempera paint or a few drops of food coloring. Or mix flour and cold water into a paste. Then add food coloring or powdered tempera paint on the paper as you paint.

Soap Paint—Put ½ cup (120 ml) cold water into a bowl and add 1 cup (237 ml) soap flakes (not laundry soap powder). Add food coloring or powdered tempera. Mix thoroughly. This paint dries with a three-dimensional effect. Glitter will adhere to the paint if it is sprinkled on while the paint is still wet. Use this paint on heavy paper or light cardboard. When cleaning up, do not pour this paint down the sink because it will clog the drain.

Squeeze Bottle Paint—Mix 1 cup (237 ml) of flour and 1 cup (237 ml) of salt. Add enough poster paint to make a paste. Pour the mixture into plastic squeeze bottles. Squeeze paint onto heavy paper or lightweight cardboard.

Clay Day

Play, play every day.
Play, play with your clay.

Overture

Because a four-year-old's control over his hands is growing, arts and crafts will be more fun for him now. Modeling is a favorite for many preschoolers. Watch and you will see what kinds of craft materials your child likes best. Encourage all of his creative works.

Performance

Play: To provide your preschooler with creative clay crafts, make available a variety of kinds of clay.
What you will need: Salt clay or play dough
How to play: When molding, provide a rolling pin, cookie cutters, and other kitchen gadgets for shaping the dough. On other occasions, encourage your child to mold the shapes with just his hands and imagination.

Finale

To provide your preschooler with creative clay crafts, encourage him to help you make the clay. (See two additional play clay recipes on page 22.)

Salt Clay—Mix ¾ cup (177 ml) salt, 2 cups (474 ml) flour, ½ teaspoon (2.5 ml) alum in a bowl. Gradually add ¾ cups (180 ml) water. Stir until the dough forms a ball. Then knead the dough. Add water if the dough is too crumbly. After molding, this clay can be baked. Set the oven to 300° F (150° C) and bake small shapes for 30 or 40 minutes or until hard.

Play Dough—In a heavy saucepan, mix 1 cup (237 ml) of flour, ½ cup (118 ml) salt, 1 teaspoon (5 ml) cream of tarter, 1 tablespoon (15 ml) oil, and 1 cup (240 ml) of water. Add a few drops of food coloring. Mix and cook over medium heat, stirring constantly until the dough leaves the sides of the saucepan. Let cool, then knead for a few minutes.

Encore

Take your child to museums to see sculptures. Also visit parks and public buildings where large metal, marble, or other kinds of sculptures are available for viewing.

          © Instructional Fair • TS Denison

Paper Weavings

Make three-fourths of a cross, and a circle complete;
And let two semicircles on a perpendicular meet.

Overture

Arts and crafts not only help your child improve many fine-motor skills, it is also an opportunity for her to express her creativity. In addition, creating crafts will be a boost to her self-esteem. Watch, and you will see certain talents emerging through her art, but do not push her in one particular direction. Provide many avenues for her creativity.

Performance

Play: For an endless array of crafts, provide a variety of kinds of paper for your child to use.
What you will need: Rolls of shelf paper, sheets of copier paper, construction paper, paper bags, tissue paper, aluminum foil, gift wrap, newspapers, old magazines, discarded wallpaper sample books, etc.
How to play: Four-year-olds have the coordination to complete many easy paper crafts. Begin with simple paper weavings. Fold one sheet of paper in half and cut from the fold to the edge of the paper, stopping 1" (25 mm) from the edges. Make three or four slits. Then weave 2" (51 mm) paper strips in and out of the slits.

Finale

Use the holidays/seasons to inspire ideas for other paper crafts, such as:
- ◆ January—Tear white construction paper circles to make snowpeople.
- ◆ February—Use heart-shapes to trace and cut out paper valentines.
- ◆ March—Cut oval shapes and decorate with paint, markers, stickers, and glitter to resemble colorful Easter eggs.
- ◆ April—Use a variety of colored construction paper cutouts, tissue paper, or facial tissues to fold into flowers petals.
- ◆ May—Use paper to make little baskets.
- ◆ June—Make paper crowns, hats, or bonnets. Decorate with glitter, feathers, or flowers.
- ◆ July—Weave paper place mats for a picnic.
- ◆ August—Cut and paste shapes on construction paper to make interesting flags/banners.
- ◆ September—Fold paper to make paper airplanes.
- ◆ October—Color or paint lunch-size paper bags orange. Stuff with newspapers and tie at the top with yarn. Decorate them to look like jack-o-lanterns.
- ◆ November—Stuff brown bags with newspapers and decorate them to look like turkeys.
- ◆ December—Fold and cut white paper to make snowflakes.

Encore

There is no end to the projects your child can make with paper. Teaching her how to cut, tear, fold, score, and wad paper will inspire her creativity.

Cutting and Pasting

Clipping and snipping, never waste.
Stick 'em together with glue or paste.
Take your time, no need for haste.

Overture

Watch to see if your preschooler is interested in cutting and pasting. Children this age are imaginative and abstract in their artwork. Cutting and pasting gives preschoolers the opportunity to rearrange parts into a new whole.

Performance

Play: To provide your preschooler with cutting and pasting crafts, assemble a craft box or plastic tub to hold his art supplies. The box should contain crayons, watercolor markers, watercolor paints, paintbrushes, play clay, blunt scissors, and glue sticks.

What you will need: Construction paper, blunt-tip scissors, glue sticks

How to play: Cutting and pasting shapes to make geometrical-shaped collages is fun and easy. Try using the secondary colors: orange, green, and purple. Cut shapes from two of the colors and paste them on a sheet of paper that is the third color. Try using all three secondary colors as the background. Which color combinations does your child like best?

Examples:
- ◆ Green and purple on orange paper
- ◆ Green and orange on purple paper
- ◆ Orange and purple on green paper

Also encourage your child to work with the primary colors (red, yellow, blue) in exactly the same way. When using primary colors or secondary colors, identify them as such by naming them for your child.

Finale

Collages are great paper and paste projects that are easy for four-year-olds. Have your child cut out pictures from old magazines. Overlap pictures on a large sheet of lightweight cardboard until your child is satisfied with the arrangement. Then glue the pictures in place with a glue stick. Encourage your child to create collages with themes such as animals, people, or sports, or work with pictures of things that are the same color, shape, etc.

Encore

If your child uses a lot of paste, have him help you make some homemade paste.

Flour Paste—Mix ¼ cup (59 ml) flour and ⅙ cup (40 ml) water with a drop of peppermint oil. Stir until the paste is creamy. Store in a plastic container with a lid.

Cornstarch Paste—In a saucepan, mix ¾ cup (177 ml) water, 2 tablespoons (30 ml) light corn syrup, and 1 teaspoon (5 ml) vinegar. Bring the mixture to a full boil. Mix ¼ cup (118 ml) cornstarch and ¾ cup (177 ml) water together. Add slowly to the boiling mixture. Stir constantly to avoid lumps. This mixture needs to stand for 24 hours before using.

Keeping Track

Milestone	Date	Comments
Can tell and understand jokes		
Can be inventive in fantasy play		
Enjoys pantomiming		
Uses large objects as props in fantasy play		
Can pantomime animals		
Can provide sound effects for stories		
Enjoys dressing up in grown-up clothes		
Enjoys watching/ using puppets		
Enjoys making crafts using paints		
Enjoys making crafts using clay		
Enjoys making crafts using paper		
Can cut and paste objects		

Think Tank

Cognitive Development

Contemplate

There are many paths of learning. Whatever path your child prefers, you can enrich his education by stimulating his senses. Talking, listening, seeing, and touching are all ways your child will learn. The more of his senses you can involve in games and activities, the more he will comprehend and remember.

The cycle of seasons and holidays that is completed each year is a wonderful motivator for young learners. Celebrations and rituals are peak experiences for children at this age. Take note of the seasons with walks to discover how the world is changing. Highlight each holiday with games, stories, crafts, and special foods. Have your own family rituals and traditions that will enrich your child's world. Use the games and activities in this chapter to advance your preschooler's cognitive skills.

Cognitive Milestones: Four Years

◆ Will learn to recognize and name primary and secondary colors
◆ Will understand the time concepts "today," "yesterday," and "tomorrow"
◆ Will understand the sequencing of events
◆ Will begin to name some of the letters of the alphabet
◆ Will be able to listen to and follow directions
◆ Will be able to retell simple stories
◆ May begin to read a few words
◆ Will learn how to count from one to twelve
◆ Will be able to recognize and name some numerals
◆ Will be able to develop a control system for his impulses
◆ Will learn to accept disciplinary actions and respond accordingly
◆ Will be able to do much of his own self-care
◆ Will be particularly responsive to social stimulation
◆ Will be particularly responsive to intellectual stimulation

© Instructional Fair • TS Denison

General Tips

The more personal the learning the more quickly a preschooler can master a concept. The more she brings to the learning, the more fun she will have with it. When teaching four-year-olds, involving the five senses is important. When playing games ask your child to tell you how things feel, smell, look, sound, etc. Engaging questions will take her learning one step further.

Appropriate books for developing a preschooler's cognitive skills include:

◆ *Barnyard Banter* by Denise Fleming (Holt, 1994)

◆ *Eating and Tasting* by Henry Arthur Pluckrose (Raintree/Steck Vaughn, 1998)

◆ *Feeling Things* by Allan Fowler (Children's Press, 1991)

◆ *Hand, Hand, Fingers, Thumb* by Al Perkins (Random House, 1969)

◆ *Hearing Things* by Allan Fowler (Children's Press, 1991)

◆ *Look! Look! Look!* by Tana Hobin (Greenwillow, 1988)

◆ *My Five Senses* by Aliki (HarperTrophy, 1990)

◆ *The Noisy Book* by Margaret Wise Brown (Harper, 1939) (Look for other "Noisy" titles: *The Indoor Noisy Book* [HarperCollins, 1994], *The Quiet Noisy Book* [Harper, 1950], and *The Winter Noisy Book,* [HarperCollins, 1994].)

◆ *Sniffing and Smelling* by Henry Arthur Pluckrose (Raintree/Steck Vaughn, 1998)

◆ *What Do You See When You Shut Your Eyes?* by Cynthia Zarin (Houghton Mifflin, 1998)

◆ *You Smell and Taste and Feel and See and Hear* by Mary Murphy (DK Pub Merchandise, 1997)

Name That Color

Daffy-Down-Dilly has come up to town,
In a purple petticoat and a green gown.
—Adapted Traditional Rhyme

Overture

By age four, most children know the names of many colors. Preschoolers have favorite colors and tend to choose clothes based on the colors of the garments rather than the style, texture, or fashion. Watch when your child gets to choose what he will wear, and you will soon discover what his favorite color is.

Performance

Play: To encourage your preschooler to recognize and name the primary (red, blue, yellow) and secondary (purple, yellow, green) colors, play "Name That Color."
What you will need: Box of 10 crayons
How to play: Arrange the crayons on a table between you and your four-year-old. Begin playing the game by naming a color and having your child pick out the appropriate crayon. It will be very easy to see which of the colors he has trouble naming. When your child knows the names of all of the crayons, play a version of the same game. Pick up a crayon and have your child name the color. As your child gets good at this game, you can use a box of 16 or 24 crayons, and teach him additional colors, such as pink, gold, silver, black, white, brown, etc.

Finale

When you are coloring with your child, discuss the picture and colors used. Make comments such as:
- ◆ You colored the horse "brown" very carefully.
- ◆ The big, "red" barn is very colorful.
- ◆ You colored the grass "green." It looks good.

At a different time as your child is coloring, ask him to describe the object and the color he is using. On other occasions, as you drive around town, ask him to point to something red, blue, or yellow. See if he can spot a "red" truck, a "green" van, or a "white" car. When you see a billboard with large letters, ask him what color the letter "A" is, etc.

Encore

Books that are appropriate for teaching a four-year-old colors include:
- ◆ *Ant and Bee and the Rainbow* by Angela Banner (Franklin Watts, 1988)
- ◆ *Colors Everywhere* by Tana Hoban (Greenwillow, 1995)
- ◆ *The Great Blueness and Other Predicaments* by Arnold Lobel (Harper & Row, 1984)
- ◆ *Growing Colors* by Bruce McMillan (Mulberry Books, 1994)
- ◆ *Is it red? Is it yellow? Is it blue? An Adventure in Color* by Tana Hoban (Greenwillow, 1978)
- ◆ *Of Colors and Things* by Tana Hoban (Mulberry Books, 1996)
- ◆ *Richard Scarry's Color Book* by Richard Scarry (Random House, 1976)

When?

Tip, top, tower,
Tumble down in an hour.

Overture

To teach a four-year-old about time, it is important to make the games as personal as possible. Talking about what happened to your child "yesterday," what is happening "today," and what may happen "tomorrow" puts time in a context that your child can understand. Watch when you use such terms to see if she understands or if the terms are too vague for her to comprehend what you are describing.

Performance

Play: To help your preschooler begin to understand the time concepts "today," "yesterday," and "tomorrow," play "When?"

What you will need: No special equipment is needed for this game; it is a conversation.

How to play: Sit with your child. Begin by introducing the concepts with examples:
- ◆ "Yesterday" is the time before you went to bed last night.
- ◆ "Today" is right now. You and I are here. Now is today.
- ◆ "Tomorrow" will come after you go to bed tonight.

Tell your child about personal events and ask, "When? Today? Yesterday? Or tomorrow?" Examples:
- ◆ We brushed our teeth, and then I put you to bed. You went to sleep. When was that?
- ◆ I asked you if you wanted to play a game, and we went outside and threw the ball back and forth. When was that?
- ◆ We are sitting here now and talking. When is that?
- ◆ You will wake up and get dressed. We will play games and have lunch. When will that be?

Finale

Use a large sheet of paper. Fold it into three parts. Write "Yesterday," "Today," and "Tomorrow" across the top of the paper. Have your child tell you some things she did yesterday. Write a word or draw a picture for each event. Then have her tell you some things you did today. Again write a word or draw a picture for each event. Finally, have her tell you some things she would like to do tomorrow. List or draw pictures of those things, too. Then review by naming the things and having her tell you if it happened "yesterday," "today," or may happen "tomorrow."

Encore

Books that will help your four-year-old learn the concept of time include:
- ◆ *Richard Scarry's Pop-Up Time* by Richard Scarry (Little Simon, 1997)
- ◆ *Telling Time with Big Mama Cat* by Dan Harper (Harcourt Brace, 1998)
- ◆ *Tick-Tock* by Lena Anderson (Farrar Straus & Giroux, 1998)
- ◆ *Wake Up, Sleep Tight* by Ken Wilson-Max (Cartwheel Books, 1998)

Before and After

Hickory, dickory, dock.
The mouse ran up the clock.
The clock struck one,
And down he run,
Hickory, dickory, dock.
—Traditional Rhyme

Overture

Watch and listen. Your child's conversations with you will tell you exactly what she understands about the sequencing of events. If she uses the past tense, present tense, and future tense of verbs, she understands time. If not, model this for her in your shared conversations.

Performance

Play: To help your child practice sequencing of events, play "Before and After."
What you will need: Two bananas
How to play: Peel one banana and leave the peeling on the other banana. Line up the banana, the peeled banana, and the peel. Ask your child to tell you a story about the bananas. Which banana represents the first part of the story? Which banana represents the middle of the story? Which part represents the end of the story? Her story might go something like this:
   ◆ A boy had a banana.
   ◆ The boy peeled the banana and ate it.
   ◆ All that was left was the peel.

Finale

On other occasions, use other household items to have your child tell you "sequence of events" stories. Include:
   ◆ Clean plate, plate with food, empty plate with food stains
   ◆ Clean glass, glass with milk, empty glass with milk stains
   ◆ A coloring book page, crayon and part of a picture colored, picture completely colored
   ◆ Sheet of paper, scissors and paper folded to make a snowflake, a paper snowflake
Place the three objects in random order. Have your child line up the objects in the correct order. Then have her tell you a story about the objects.

Encore

Ask your child questions that require her to sequence events.
   ◆ Which comes first, morning or night?
   ◆ Which do we eat last, breakfast or dinner?
   ◆ What is at the end of a train, the engine or caboose?
   ◆ Which comes first on a car, the headlights or taillights?
   ◆ Which do you put on first, shoes or socks?
   ◆ When icing a cake, do you put the frosting on before or after you bake the cake?
   ◆ When you go to sleep, which do you do last: close your eyes, climb into bed, or pull up the covers?

          © Instructional Fair • TS Denison

Naming the Alphabet

Great A, little a,
bouncing B!
The cat's in the cupboard,
And can't see me.
—Traditional Rhyme

Overture

Watch, and you may see that your child can name some of the letters of the alphabet. There is no hurry to teach your preschooler to read; however, many preschoolers learn to read on their own. Words on signs like "Stop" or icons for fast-food restaurants may be among your child's first reading vocabulary.

Performance

Play: To introduce your preschooler to letters of the alphabet, play with alphabet flash cards.

What you will need: Flash cards (you can make these on index cards or purchase cards with pictures)

How to play: Choose a letter of the alphabet such as the first letter of your child's name. At this stage, do not overwhelm your child with more than a few letters. Show him the card. Ask him to trace the letter with his index finger. Beginning at the top of the letter, guide his hand in touching each line of the letter. Say the name of the letter as your child traces it.

Finale

Another way of tracing the letters of the alphabet is to write them in a large size on paper and have your child outline them with a crayon. Do not frustrate him by introducing more than two or three letters during a session. Make sure the letters are big enough for him to easily trace.

Encore

If magnetic letters are available, display the letters on the front of your refrigerator and invite your child to play with them. Simple words can be created with the letters, such as mom, dad, me, cat, etc. If you have any magnetic animal shapes, form the corresponding words for the shapes. Encourage your child to think of different ways to play with the letters.

Alphabet Break

A, B, C, and D,
Play, playmates, agree.
E, F, and G,
Well, so it shall be.

Overture

Many parents of four-year-olds feel pressured to begin teaching their youngster to read and write. Do not overdo teaching letters and numbers. There is no hurry. As your child shows an interest in learning certain letters and numbers, play games using those particular letters or numbers. Watch for clues that he is interested and wants to learn these things.

Performance

Play: To practice letter recognition and following directions, play "Alphabet Break."
What you will need: Half sheets of paper, wide-tip black marker
How to play: On a half sheet of paper, print an uppercase letter of the alphabet. Give your child the paper with the letter. Give verbal directions, such as:
- ◆ Hold up "A" and stand up.
- ◆ Hold letter "A" high over your head.
- ◆ Put the letter "A" on your head.
- ◆ Hand me the letter "A."
- ◆ Stand up and march around with the letter "A." Stop. Sit down.
- ◆ Stand up and hold the letter "A" behind your back.

Finale

After your child has played the game with one letter of the alphabet, introduce another letter card and use both to play the game. After awhile have him give you directions to follow with the same alphabet cards. Continue to add new alphabet cards. When your child knows the whole alphabet, play an advanced version of this game using all 26 letters of the alphabet.

Encore

Practice the alphabet by singing the "A-B-C" song (the tune is "Twinkle, Twinkle, Little Star"). Appropriate books for teaching preschoolers about the alphabet include:
- ◆ *26 Letters and 99 Cents* by Tana Hoban (Greenwillow, 1988)
- ◆ *Dr. Seuss's ABC: Beginner Books* by Dr. Seuss (Random House, 1996)
- ◆ *Curious George Learns the Alphabet* by H. A. Rey (Houghton Mifflin, 1973)
- ◆ *Brian Wildsmith's ABC (Board Book)* by Brian Wildsmith (Star Bright Books, 1996)

        © Instructional Fair • TS Denison

Tell Me the Story

Tell me a story,
An old or new story.

Overture

Four-year-olds are old enough to sit and listen to long stories. For a child this age, made-up stories about family members are especially enjoyable. Your child will love hearing stories about you when you were her age. Watch her face as you tell her stories about the childhoods of all your family members.

Performance

Play: To help your preschooler learn how to retell a story, play "Tell Me the Story."
What you will need: Picture books with simple stories are especially good for retelling.
How to play: Choose picture books with repeated events and words. Showing the pictures, read or tell the story once. Then turn the pages of the book and look at the pictures as your child tells you the story. On another occasion, ask your child to "read" the story to you. She might only give you one or two words per page, and that is okay. Reread the book to her and then ask her to read it to you again. The more familiar she becomes with the text, the more parts of the story she will be able to retell.

Finale

To boost your child's listening and comprehension skills, ask questions after you read a story. Especially, ask questions that test to see if your child understands the sequence of events. For example, after telling the story "The Three Bears," you may ask questions such as:
- ◆ What was the first thing Goldilocks did when she went into the bears' house?
- ◆ Did Goldilocks eat porridge or take a nap first?
- ◆ Did Goldilocks take a nap or sit in the chairs first?
- ◆ Which of the beds did Goldilocks try last?
- ◆ Which sized chair did Goldilocks try last?
- ◆ Whose chair did Goldilocks sit in first?

Encore

To encourage your child to learn from stories, follow these few rules:
- ◆ When your child asks questions during a story, do not stifle her. Answer her questions, and tell her how proud you are that she is thinking about the story.
- ◆ As your child is expanding her language and thinking by hearing and speaking words, encourage her to talk about the stories.
- ◆ Stimulate your child intellectually without pushing her. How your child reacts to a game will let you know whether she is bored or challenged beyond her interests.

Word Cards

"A" for apples sold at the fair.
"B" for bananas, we bought some there.

Overture..

Watch, and you will probably discover that your child recognizes some words already. Words that she sees every day such as "Stop" on road signs and "Exit" in public buildings are probably words that she can recognize. As you read simple story books to your child, you may notice that he is very capable of reading those books to you.

Performance..

Play: To make common words available to your child, create word cards and place them in appropriate places around the house.
What you will need: Small index cards, black marker
How to play: List the names of objects found around the house and tape them in the appropriate places. Examples: door, floor, window, bed, clock, stove, refrigerator

Finale..

Use the whole alphabet to make word cards. Write the words in bold lettering and place them around your house. If your child is not familiar with one of the words, choose a different one for that letter. You may have to resort to pictures of objects when you get to the difficult letters such as "X" and "Z."

"A" is for apple.	"N" is for nuts.
"B" is for banana.	"O" is for onion.
"C" is for cauliflower.	"P" is for pudding.
"D" is for door.	"Q" is for quilt.
"E" is for egg.	"R" is for refrigerator.
"F" is for floor.	"S" is for stove.
"G" is for a gate.	"T" is for television.
"H" is for the hairbrush.	"U" is for umbrella.
"I" is for ice cream.	"V" is for vase.
"J" is for jeep.	"W" is for wagon.
"K" is for key.	"X" is for xylophone.
"L" is for lamp.	"Y" is for yo-yo.
"M" is for map.	"Z" is for zebra.

Encore..

If your child notices and is interested in learning about words on a page, provide your child with books that have simple text. Books your child may enjoy include:
- *I Read Signs* by Tana Hoban (William Morrow, 1987)
- *Richard Scarry's Early Words* by Richard Scarry (Random House, 1999)
- *Richard Scarry's Best Picture Dictionary* by Richard Scarry (Golden Books, 1998)
- *Richard Scarry's Best Little Word Book Ever!* by Richard Scarry (Golden Books, 1992)

Buckle My Shoe

One, two, buckle my shoe.
Three, four, shut the door.
Five, six, pick up sticks.
Seven, eight, lay them straight.
Nine, ten, a good fat hen.
Eleven, twelve, who will delve?
—Traditional Rhyme

Overture

Simply hearing the numbers will be all your child needs to learn them. Most four-year-olds can count while correctly pointing to three objects. Many can count to ten or twelve. Verbal counting without objects will come before her ability to count objects.

Performance

Play: To help your child learn to count from one to twelve, play "Buckle My Shoe."
What you will need: No special equipment is needed to play this game.
How to play: Begin by teaching the rhyme. Then turn the rhyme into an action game.

One, two, buckle my shoe. (*Bend over as if buckling your shoe.*)
Three, four, shut the door. (*Stand up and pretend to close a door.*)
Five, six, pick up sticks. (*Bend over and pretend to pick up sticks.*)
Seven, eight, lay them straight. (*Pretend to lay sticks straight.*)
Nine, ten, a good fat hen. (*Stand up, tuck arms like wings, and flap them.*)
Eleven, twelve, who will delve? (*Pretend to dig a hole with an imaginary shovel.*)

Finale

Use rhymes as a starting signal for running races. Teach your child these traditional rhymes and others.

Off and Away	**Go**
Bell-horses, bell-horses,	One for the money,
What time of day?	Two for the show,
One o'clock, two o'clock,	Three to make ready,
Off and away.	And four to go.

Encore

During the day, count things out loud for your child. While you read stories, have your child count different objects shown in the pictures. Try to encourage your child to count small groups of objects at various times.

◆ When you get the mail from the box, ask your child to count the pieces of mail.
◆ When your child is picking up toys, ask her to count the balls and so on.
◆ When you are brushing your child's hair, count the strokes.
◆ When you and your child are setting the table for a meal, count the plates, forks, spoons, and so on. This is an excelllent opportunity to practice one-to-one correspondence.

Counting Rhymes

1, 2, 3, 4, 5!
I caught a hare alive;
6, 7, 8, 9, 10!
I let it go again.
         —Traditional Rhyme

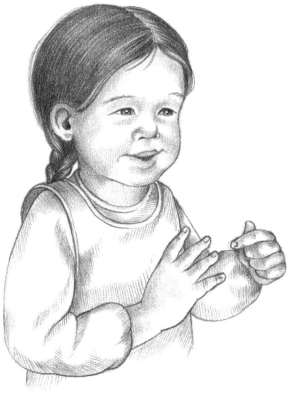

Overture ....

Watch, and you will see your child learning stories more quickly when they are part of a rhyme or song.

Performance ....

Play: To help your child learn to recognize and name numerals, use counting rhymes.

What you will need: No special equipment is needed for this game.

How to play: Learn counting rhymes for signaling a race or as blue-bells jump rope rhyme. For example, such as the traditional rhyme:

Mary
One, two, three, four,
Mary at the cottage door;
Five, six, seven, eight,
Eating cherries off a plate;
O-U-T spells out!

Finale...

Use rhymes for finger plays. The following rhymes not only stimulate listening skills but emphasize simple mathematics.

Captain and Men
1, 2, 3, 4, 5 in a row.
(Pop up fingers one at a time on right hand.)
A captain and his men!
And on the other side, you know,
Are 6, 7, 8, 9, 10.
(Pop up fingers one at a time on left hand.)
         —Louis Binder Scott

Counting at the Farm
One, one. A farm is lots of fun.
Two, two. Hear the kitten mew.
Three, three. Birds are in a tree.
Four, four. Hear the puppy snore.
Five, five. Bees buzz in a hive.
(Hold up the required number of fingers each time.)
         —Louis Binder Scott

Encore...

When reciting a counting rhyme, pause and see if your child can fill in the next number or word.

© Instructional Fair • TS Denison

Time Out!

Little Tom Twig bought a fine bow and arrow,
And what did he shoot? Why, a poor little sparrow. . . .
—Traditional Rhyme

Overture

Watch your four-year-old and you may see what is described as "out-of-bounds" behavior. Full of energy, children at this age are sometimes rough, impatient, and quarrelsome. They sometimes act out without thinking. It may become necessary for you to sit your child down so he can have time to get calm, think, and recenter.

Performance

Play: To help your child develop a control system for his impulses, have "Time Outs."

What you will need: No special equipment is needed for this activity.

How to play: "Time Outs" do not have to be treated like punishment, but rather they should be viewed as a time to put on the brakes and safely go in a new direction. Begin by talking to your child about how cars have to slow down before they can turn corners. Explain how braking makes a new direction possible. Let your child pick a sound that will signal a time for his "Time Outs." It might be a whistle, horn, bell on a timer, or a secret word. Encourage your child to help you write the rules for the "Time Outs." The more input he has in the planning, the more likely he will be to follow the rules. Make up your own rules such as:

◆ When you hear the bell you have (certain amount of time) to go to the chosen spot.
◆ The chosen spot for "Time Outs" is _____.
◆ When you get to the chosen spot, you cannot _____.
◆ When you are having "Time Out," you may _____.
◆ The signal that "Time Out" is over is _____.

Finale

Another approach to "Time Outs" is to make it a make-believe fantasy game.

◆ Lie flat on your back on your bed and pretend you are floating around on a cloud.
◆ Sit cross-legged and with hands in your lap, close your eyes and hum like a busy beehive.
◆ On your bed, lie on your stomach and pretend to be a jellyfish floating on the sea.
◆ Sitting on your bed, with your legs folded up under you, see how long you can sit perfectly still. Listen for the sound of something outside of the house.

Encore

Using "Time Outs" as punishment teaches children that stopping and getting quiet and calm is negative. If you use Time Outs as a reward, you will be giving your child the gift of being able to get centered and calm. It is important to teach your child how to slow down and become relaxed.

Whispering Voices

Shhhhhhhh

Overture ....

By nature, four-year-olds tend to be very loud and boisterous. They can be very difficult to handle, especially in the evenings. Watch to see if your child gets louder and louder as the day grows longer.

Performance ....

Play: To get your child to calm down and listen, play a game where everyone talks in a whisper.

What you will need: No special equipment is needed to play this game.

How to play: If your child is very loud and will not pay attention to what you are saying, whisper to her. Make eye contact so she knows you are talking to her and whisper your instructions. No matter how loud she is, only communicate with her in a whisper. Whisper that you want him to whisper to you. You might set up a secret signal that means only whispering voices can be used for a short period of time. Set a timer for five or ten minutes. Whispering will help your child learn how to communicate quietly.

Finale ....

To help your preschooler accept disciplinary actions and respond accordingly, include her in the making of rules. For a child to obey rules, she needs to have only a few, and they should be rules that protect your child.

Examples:
- ◆ No running into the street.
- ◆ Must hold an adult's hand while crossing the street.
- ◆ Can only climb the tree in the backyard when with an adult.
- ◆ Never play with fire.

List the rules your child helps you create. Post them where everyone can see them.

Encore ....

It is important to establish what will happen if a rule is broken. Here are some helpful tips:
- ◆ Consequences for breaking the rules should be clearly defined. Example: If you do this, then this is what will happen.
- ◆ Choose consequences that make sense and are related to the misbehavior. Example: If you run into the street, you cannot play in the front yard for three days.
- ◆ Consequences for breaking rules should be consistent. Do not adhere to the rules one day and not the next. Mixed signals may cause your child to think, "Well, nothing happened yesterday, so I can probably get away with it again today."
- ◆ If at all possible, let your child help you set up fair consequences for breaking the rules.

        © Instructional Fair • TS Denison

Take Care

As I walked by myself, and talked to myself,
Myself said unto me,
Look to thyself, take care of thyself, . . .
—Traditional Rhyme

Overture

Watch your four-year-old, and you will see that she is making rapid progress toward complete independence in self-care.

Performance

Activity: To encourage your child's self-care, provide appropriate tools.
What you will need: Child-sized comb and hairbrush, toothpaste and toothbrush, step stool
How to play: Have a special place in the bathroom for your child to keep her self-care tools.

◆ Make sure she has her own comb and brush.
◆ Make sure she has her own toothpaste and toothbrush.
◆ Make sure her clothes are hung on low rods and dresser drawers can be easily pulled out.
◆ Make sure she has shoes that buckle or close with Velcro and do not need to be tied.
◆ Make sure she has a stool to stand on so she can reach things in the bathroom.

Finale

To encourage your child to take a bath independently:

◆ Be nearby but still provide privacy.
◆ Fill the tub to the correct level for her.
◆ Make sure she knows which tap is hot water and is instructed never to turn on that faucet.
◆ Place a nonslip mat in the bathtub for getting in and out of the bath.
◆ Make sure soap, a wash cloth, and a towel are where they can be reached.
◆ Provide bath toys to be used in the tub.

Encore

To encourage your child to have table manners:

◆ Encourage conversation and include her during the meal.
◆ Do not make the mealtime too long.
◆ If your child has trouble sitting still long enough to eat, do not put her in a stressful situation.
◆ Make sure your child has child-sized utensils.
◆ Explain the table rules: Do not talk with food in your mouth. Do not play with your food.

Peer Pressure

Georgey Porgey, pudding and pie,
Kissed the girls and made them cry.
When the girls come out to play,
Georgey Porgey runs away.
—Traditional Rhyme

Overture

Preschoolers are much more interactive with peers than ever before. Watch and you will see that your four-year-old learns more from socializing with peers than he could ever learn from being at home. Make sure your preschooler has play time with children his age.

Performance

Play: To provide social stimulation, make sure your preschooler spends time with peers.
What you will need: Playground where there are children, play group, or preschool
How to play: Four-year-olds should spend an hour or two several times a week with children their own age. More frequent, short gatherings are better than longer ones. When your child is playing with other children, listen to his play but do not interfere or direct it.

Finale

Peers offer your child an opportunity to solve problems on his own. Aggression and experimenting with ways to deal with it are part of his learning. Talking to your child about his feelings and giving him good examples of how to deal with problems are the most important ways to strengthen his social skills. He will not remember what you say, but he will remember what you do.

◆ Do not yell at your child for being noisy.
◆ Do not spank your child for being aggressive.
◆ Do not ignore your child because he will not listen.

Encore

The key to successful play groups or gatherings of four-year-olds is to make games and activities simple. A variety of games is important because four-year-olds lose interest quickly. For variety, spend part of the time indoors and part of the time outside.

        © Instructional Fair • TS Denison

Field Trips

Take a bus; take a plane.
Take a boat; take a train.

Overture......................................

The more exposure your child has to interesting places, the more stimulated she will be intellectually and socially. Watch when you take your child to new and interesting places; you will see her in the optimal learning environment.

Performance.................................

Play: To stimulate your child's cognitive growth, take her on outings.
What you will need: Transportation, camera
How to play: Try to visit a new and interesting place at least once a month. Take a few photographs of each outing. Make a scrapbook and talk to your child about the places you visit. Some ideas include:

- ◆ Swim in a lake, pond, ocean, or public pool
- ◆ Ride on a bus, train, or boat
- ◆ Visit a farm, zoo, or pet store
- ◆ Play at a friend's house
- ◆ Go to the fair or circus
- ◆ Watch a puppet show
- ◆ Attend a concert or ballet
- ◆ Spend time at a museum

Finale ....

Use educational videos to teach your child about history and nature. Documentaries and science videos produced for children are educational and entertaining. Find out what your child is most interested in and give her many opportunities to learn all about that topic.

Encore ....

Use your public library to stimulate your child intellectually, too. Join a story group and bring books home. Visiting the library may become a weekly outing that will be enjoyed by you and your child.

Keeping Track

Milestone	Date	Comments
Recognizes and names various colors		
Understands time concepts: "today," "yesterday," "tomorrow"		
Can sequence story events		
Can name some letters of the alphabet		
Can listen to and follow directions		
Can retell a simple story		
Can read a few basic words		
Can count from one to twelve		
Can recognize and name some numerals		
Has developed a control system for impulses		
Can calm him/herself and listen		
Has many self-care skills		
Is responsive to social stimulation		
Is responsive to intellectual stimulation		

© Instructional Fair • TS Denison